AMERICAN INDIANS OF THE PLATEAU AND PLAINS

NATIVE AMERICAN TRIBES

AMERICAN INDIANS OF THE PLATEAU AND PLAINS

EDITED BY KATHLEEN KUIPER, MANAGER, ARTS AND CULTURE

Britannica®
Educational Publishing

IN ASSOCIATION WITH

ROSEN
EDUCATIONAL SERVICES

Published in 2012 by Britannica Educational Publishing
(a trademark of Encyclopædia Britannica, Inc.)
in association with Rosen Educational Services, LLC
29 East 21st Street, New York, NY 10010.

First Edition

Britannica Educational Publishing
Michael I. Levy: Executive Editor
J.E. Luebering: Senior Manager
Marilyn L. Barton: Senior Coordinator, Production Control
Steven Bosco: Director, Editorial Technologies
Lisa S. Braucher: Senior Producer and Data Editor
Yvette Charboneau: Senior Copy Editor
Kathy Nakamura: Manager, Media Acquisition
Kathleen Kuiper: Manager, Arts and Culture

Rosen Educational Services
Hope Lourie Killcoyne: Executive Editor
Nelson Sá: Art Director
Cindy Reiman: Photography Manager
Karen Huang: Photo Researcher
Brian Garvey: Designer
Matthew Cauli: Cover Design
Introduction by Kathleen Kuiper

Library of Congress Cataloging-in-Publication Data

American Indians of the Plateau and Plains/edited by Kathleen Kuiper.
    p. cm.—(Native American tribes)
"In association with Britannica Educational Publishing, Rosen Educational Services."
Includes bibliographical references and index.
ISBN 978-1-61530-689-3 (library binding)
1. Indians of North America—Great Plains—History. 2. Indians of North America—
Great Plains—Social life and customs. I. Kuiper, Kathleen.
E78.G73A48 2012
978.00497—dc23

                                                          2011028730

Manufactured in the United States of America

On the cover: Nez Percé man on his Appaloosa, preparing to ride to the Bear Paw
Mountains of Montana. It was there in 1877 that U.S. troops surrounded Chief Joseph and
his followers, putting an end to the long and dramatic but ultimately failed attempt of the
Nez Percé band to reach Canada. *Marilyn Angel Wynn/Nativestock/Getty Images*

On pages viii-ix: After its introduction in the 18th century, the horse became integral to
Native Americans of the Plateau and Plains. This group from the Apsaroka (Crow) tribe—
a chief and his scouts on horseback—was photographed by Edward S. Curtis, *c.* 1905.
Library of Congress Prints and Photographs Division

On pages 1, 19, 31, 44, 73, 83, 111, 133, 134, 137, 140: Nineteenth-century colourized
engraving depicting members of the Blackfoot tribe hunting buffalo, Three Buttes,
Montana. *Stock Montage/Archive Photos/Getty Images*

CONTENTS

4

24

39

INTRODUCTION

All religions have lines their adherents must not cross. For the Nez Percé, a tribe of Plateau Indians, one of these lines was the eating of salmon before the first salmon ceremony. When the first fish of the season was landed, the people celebrated. As in a Passover Seder, a Roman Catholic Mass, or the Muslim festivity called 'Īd al-Aḍḥā certain things had to be done in a certain way. For the first salmon ceremony, the fish was cooked over an open fire. The people drank water to purify their bodies before accepting what was considered the gift of the Creator.

Specific songs were sung, and food was prepared and served according to tradition on mats made of bulrushes and placed on the floor. After the drinking of water, a portion of the first fish was parceled out to each of the celebrants. Then a succession of other foods that were part of the Nez Percé diet were eaten in a fixed order. It was then the custom to return all of the fish bones, unbroken, to the river so that the salmon could regenerate and return again. In this way children learned their traditions and witnessed their people's deep respect for everyone, including the creatures that helped them to survive.

Salmon was and remains a culture hero—a figure of legend who shifted shapes and was both human and fish. Though many traditional fishing grounds have since been degraded and partly ruined by pollutants and erosion or drowned by dams, the Nez Percé continue to celebrate their past and to honour nature in the present. Salmon continues to provide nourishment for his people.

The Nez Percé are among the peoples living in what anthropologists and others consider to be the Plateau culture area. (A culture area is defined as a contiguous geographic region within which most societies share many traits—such as language, religion, and other ways of life.) The other culture area treated in this volume is the Plains.

The European conquest of North America took place in fits and starts from the Atlantic and Pacific coasts toward the continent's interior. Even during the early colonial period, the Plains and the Plateau peoples were affected by epidemics of foreign diseases and a slow influx of European trade goods. But the Indian nations of the interior did not have sustained direct interaction with the colonizers until the 18th century.

In 1738 the Mandan villages on the upper Missouri River hosted a party led by the French trader Pierre Gaultier de Varennes et de la Vérendrye. This event is often said to have started the lasting contact between the peoples of the northern Plains and the colonial powers. Certainly a significant number of traders, such as the English explorer David Thompson, were living with Plains peoples by the late 18th century. According to the letters and diaries of these traders, the interior nations were adept negotiators who enjoyed a relatively prosperous lifestyle. Indeed, many visitors commented on the luxury they found in the Plains earth lodges. Although somewhat less historical data exists for the Plateau peoples of this era, it is clear that the 18th century was a time of great change for both groups. The introduction of three items—horses, guns, and peoples from adjacent culture areas—was responsible for the particular trajectory of change in these regions.

Horses had been introduced to the Americas by the Spanish conquistadors. The advantages of using horses, whether as pack animals or as mounts, were obvious to the Plains and Plateau peoples, who had until then been obligated to travel overland by foot, using dogs as draft animals, or in small boats on the regions' few navigable rivers. They soon discovered that they could obtain horses in a variety of ways: through purchase or trade, by raiding, or by taming animals from the wild herds that soon arose.

Unlike the groups who inhabited the dense forests of the Northeast, Southeast, and Subarctic, the peoples of the Plateau and Plains had vast areas of grassland and desert that encouraged the horse culture. As a result of geography then, horses spread from the Southwest culture area to the Plains and the Plateau following a northerly and easterly trajectory. As the possession and exploitation of horses spread, they were rapidly included in buffalo hunts. Before the horse, such hunts had been dangerous affairs: the range of the bow and arrow was small, requiring hunters to get nearer to these enormous and powerful animals than was prudent. Alternatively they could stampede a herd of buffalo toward a cliff and cause them to fall to their deaths. The horse's speed and mobility proved to be a great advantage to the hunters, providing (if nothing else) a means of escaping the fury of a wounded animal.

As to guns, Spanish law expressly forbade the distribution of firearms to indigenous individuals, but the English and Dutch traded these weapons freely. Initially used in battle and to hunt the large game of the eastern and boreal forests, firearms were readily incorporated into the buffalo hunt. Both the horse's speed and maneuverability and the rifle's firepower granted more distance between hunter and hunted and lessened the danger of attack from a charging animal.

Horses and guns spread to the interior over the course of about 100 years, from roughly 1600 to 1700. By approximately 1700 many tribes were moving to the interior as well. Those from the Northeast were farming groups pushed west by the intertribal hostilities of the Huron-Algonquian-French and Iroquois-English alliances. Those from the Southwest were Apachean and other hunters and gatherers who, having acquired horses, were able for the first time to match the movement of the buffalo herds. By the 1750s the horse culture of the southern interior had met with the gun culture of the northern interior. From the mid-18th century to the first part of the 19th century, horses and guns enabled the indigenous nations of the North American interior to enjoy a level of prosperity they had not known before.

Lying at the crossroads of five culture areas (the Subarctic, Plains, Great Basin, California, and Northwest Coast), the Plateau is surrounded by mountains and drained by two great river systems (the Fraser and the Columbia). It is situated in present-day Montana, Idaho, Oregon, Washington, and British Columbia. The topography of the area is characterized by rolling hills, high flatlands, gorges, and mountain slopes. The Plateau climate is temperate and milder than the adjacent Plains because the surrounding mountain systems provide protection from continental air masses. The mountains also create a substantial rain shadow. Most precipitation falls at higher elevations, leaving other areas rather dry. The predominant ecosystems are grassland and high desert, although there are considerable forested areas at higher altitudes.

Most of the languages spoken in this culture area belong to the Salishan, Sahaptin, Kutenai, and Modoc and Klamath families. Tribes include the Salish, Flathead, Nez Percé, Yakama, Kutenai, Modoc and Klamath, Spokan, Kalispel, Pend d'Oreille, Coeur d'Alene, Walla Walla, and Umatilla.

The village was the main political unit, though some groups possessed a sense of larger tribal and cultural unity and created representative governments, tribal chieftainships, and confederations of tribes. This was possible in part because the Columbia and Fraser rivers provided enough salmon and other fish to support a relatively dense population. But this region was never as heavily populated or as rigidly stratified as the Northwest Coast.

The peoples of the Plateau were efficient hunters and gatherers who supplemented their supplies of fish with terrestrial animals and wild plant foods. Most groups resided in permanent riverside villages and traveled upland during seasonal foraging excursions. But once horses were available, some groups shifted to nomadic buffalo hunting. These groups quickly adopted tepees and many other Plains cultural forms. They became particularly respected for their horse breeding programs and fine herds. Those who lived in fishing villages built multifamily A-frame dwellings, while smaller conical structures were typical houses in the uplands. In terms of portable culture, the Plateau peoples used a wide variety of substances and technologies. They were continuously exposed to new goods and ideas through trade with surrounding culture areas, and they excelled at material innovation and at adapting introduced technologies to their own purposes.

The Plains culture area lies in the centre of the continent, spanning the region between the western mountains and the Mississippi River valley and from the southern edge of the Subarctic to the Rio Grande in present-day Texas. It has a continental climate, with warm summers and cold winters. Relatively flat short-grass prairies with little precipitation are found west of the Missouri River, and rolling tallgrass prairies with more moisture are found to its east. Tree-lined river valleys form a series of linear oases throughout the region.

The indigenous peoples of the Plains include speakers of Siouan, Algonquian, Uto-Aztecan, Caddoan, Athabaskan, Kiowa-Tanoan, and Michif languages. Plains peoples also invented a sign language to represent common objects or concepts such as "buffalo," "battle," or "exchange."

Until the late 16th century, the only settlements on the Plains were earth-lodge villages. They were found along major waterways that provided fertile soil for growing corn, beans, squash, sunflowers, and tobacco. The groups who built these communities divided their time between farming and hunting expeditions, which often lasted for several weeks and involved travel over a considerable area.

As in the Plateau region, horses from the Spanish colonies in present-day New Mexico had become common in the Plains, their presence transforming the hunting of buffalo. This new economic opportunity caused some local villagers to become dedicated nomads, as with the Crow, and also drew agricultural tribes from surrounding areas— including the Sioux, Blackfoot, Cheyenne, Comanche, Arapaho, and Kiowa—into a nomadic lifestyle.

Groups throughout the region had in common several forms of material culture, including the tepee, tailored leather clothing, a variety of battle regalia (such as feathered headdresses), and large drums used in ritual contexts. The Sun Dance, a ritual that demanded a high degree of piety and self-sacrifice from its participants, was also found throughout most of the Plains.

The Plains may be the culture area in which tribal and band classifications were most confused. Depictions of indigenous Americans in popular culture have often been loosely based on Plains peoples, and many nonnative people consider them to be the "typical" American Indian. Of course, as readers of this detailed volume will see, there is no such thing as typical in any discussion of indigenous North Americans.

The success of the Plains Indians was much admired and also very much feared among both other native groups and settlers in the West. For a time they managed to push back the movement of settlers, nearly scuttling the notion of Manifest Destiny, the supposedly inevitable march of U.S. boundaries west to the Pacific. Yet somehow—between the destruction of buffalo herds, the introduction of disease and the Colt revolver, the settlers' learning to fight the Indian way, and the treachery of the disregarded treaties—the Indian peoples of the Plateau and Plains were brought to their knees. There are few more poignant statements of their final defeat than the surrender of Chief Joseph of the Nez Percé, who was pursued for some 1,700 miles (2,735 kilometres) before he yielded. A reporter from *Harper's Weekly* (Nov. 17, 1877) reported the event this way:

"Our [*Harper's*] artist was the only person present who committed the proceedings to writing, and took the reply as it fell from the lips of the speaker. Joseph's little girl was lost in the hills during the first day's fight, his brother was killed, his relatives dead or fugitives; he upheld now only a lost cause. His answer was:

"Tell General Howard I know his heart. What he told me before, I have it in my heart. I am tired of fighting. Our chiefs are killed; Looking Glass is dead, Ta-Hool-Hool-Shute is dead. The old men are all dead. It is the young men who say 'Yes' or 'No.' He who led on the young men is dead. It is cold, and we have no blankets; the little children are freezing to death. My people, some of them, have run away to the hills, and have no blankets, no food. No one knows where they are—perhaps freezing to death. I want to have time to look for my children, and see how many of them I can find. Maybe I shall find them among the dead. Hear me my chiefs! I am tired; my heart is sick and sad. From where the sun now stands I will fight no more forever."

Chapter 1

TRADITIONAL CULTURE OF THE PLATEAU INDIANS

The Native American peoples inhabiting the high plateau region between the Rocky Mountains and the coastal mountain system are typically referred to as Plateau Indians. The physical geography of the Plateau region is quite complex and varied. Its northern boundary consists of the low extensions of the Rocky Mountains, such as the Cariboo Mountains. The Rockies, together with the Lewis Range, also form the eastern edge. The southernmost limits are formed by the Blue Mountains and the Salmon River (excepting a narrow corridor to present-day California). The western edge is defined by the Canadian Coast Mountains and the Cascade Range. The watersheds of the Columbia and Fraser rivers are within its bounds.

A continental climate is typical of the Plateau region, with temperatures ranging from -30 °F (-34 °C) in winter to 100 °F (38 °C) in summer. Little precipitation falls there, but it usually forms a snow cover during the winter, particularly at higher altitudes. Three different vegetation types can be found in the region. The Middle Columbia area is a steppe of sagebrush and bunchgrass fringed by yellow pine on higher levels. The Upper Columbia consists mainly of wooded areas, although grassland is found in river valleys. The Fraser area is a semi-open coniferous forest occasionally interrupted by dry grassland and a partly maritime flora.

The southern boundary of the Plateau ecosystem gradually merges with the northern reaches of the Great Basin. The boundaries between the corresponding culture areas are equally imprecise. Anthropologists sometimes refer to

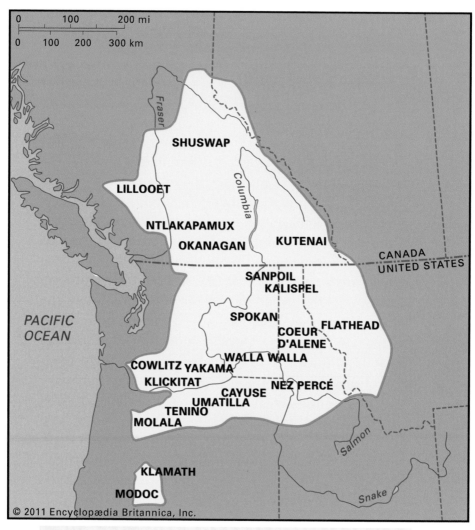

Distribution of North American Plateau Indians.

the Plateau and Great Basin jointly as the Intermontane culture area.

LANGUAGE

Speakers of four language groups—Salishan, Sahaptin, Kutenai, and Klamath-Modoc—dominate the Plateau region. The majority of Plateau languages belong to the Salishan and Sahaptin languages, and sometimes those groups are categorized under those umbrella names.

Salishan-speaking tribes may be conveniently divided into Northern Plateau and Interior (or Inland) Salish. (There are also Coast Salish languages, but these are spoken by groups classified as Northwest Coast Indians.) Of the two divisions spoken in the Plateau area, the Northern Plateau Salish include the Shuswap, Lillooet, and Ntlakapamux (Thompson) tribes. The Interior Salish, who live mostly in the Upper Columbia area, include the Okanagan, Cowlitz, Sinkaietk, Lake, Wenatchee, Sanpoil, Nespelim, Spokan, Kalispel, Pend d'Oreille, Coeur d'Alene, and Flathead peoples. Some early works incorrectly denote all Salishan groups as "Flathead."

Sahaptin speakers may be subdivided into three main groups: the Nez Percé, the Cayuse and Molala, and the Central Sahaptin, comprising the Yakama, Klickitat, Walla Walla, Tenino, Umatilla, and others.

The Kutenai and the Klamath-Modoc language families include the Kutenai and the Modoc and Klamath peoples.

CROSSROADS OF CULTURES

Because of its geographic location in the centre of four other culture areas—the Northwest Coast, the Plains, the Great Basin, and California—the Plateau constituted a crossroads of cultures. An expansive trade network enabled the exchange of goods, ideas, and even people, as slavery was common in the region. From the Northwest Coast cultures came innovations in shelters (such as mat-covered houses and pit houses), the carving of animal motifs in wood and bone, and cremation and scaffold burials, the latter of which kept the corpse from wild animals.

Kutenai woman, c. *1910*. Buyenlarge/Archive Photos/Getty Images

Part of this diffusion undoubtedly occurred through trade-based interactions, while other ideas arrived with the Wishram, a Chinook group that migrated from the Northwest Coast into the Cascade Mountains.

During the 18th century, influences from the south and east grew in importance. The Great Basin's Shoshone had acquired horses by this time and furnished their closest neighbours on the Plains and the Plateau with the new animals. The Plateau tribes placed such a high value on horses that European and Euro-American traders testified that the Nez Percé, Cayuse, Walla Walla, and Flathead had more horses than the tribes of the northern Plains from the early 19th century onward.

During the late 18th and early 19th centuries, the peoples of the Middle Columbia area adopted several kinds of material culture from the Plains. Sahaptin women, for example, made and wore Plains-inspired beaded dresses, men began to wear feathered headdresses and other war regalia, and tepees became popular. Similar innovations occurred on the eastern periphery of the Plateau, especially among the Flathead and the Kutenai. The northwestern Salishan peoples, however, rejected these changes in favour of maintaining Plateau traditions. The military ethos common among the Plains peoples was not found uniformly among residents of the Plateau. The Ntlakapamux, Shuswap, Sahaptin, and Klamath did make occasional war raids, dressed in elk hide or wooden slat armour and armed with bows and clubs. Other groups chose to avoid conflict, however. The Flathead in particular were well regarded by visitors for their courtesy, hospitality, honesty, and courage.

SHELTER

Settlements among the Plateau peoples consisted of permanent villages during the winter, with the remainder of the year divided between those villages and a variety of semipermanent camps conveniently situated for hunting and gathering. As soon as they adopted horses, however, some groups became more nomadic, using mobile camps as they traversed the Rocky Mountains in order to hunt buffalo on the Plains.

Typically, a village was home to between a few hundred and a thousand people, although the community could house even greater numbers during major events. Villages were generally located on waterways, often at rapids or narrows where fish were abundant during the winter season. Communities owned the fishing sites and surrounding area in common. Each village also had an upland for hunting. Unlike the fishing localities, upland territories were mostly open to people from other villages as well.

Two main types of housing were common in the villages, the semisubterranean pit house and the mat-covered surface house. Pit houses were usually circular and typically had a pit 3–6 feet (1–2 metres) deep and a diameter of 25–40 feet (7.5–12 m), with an interior space of approximately 500–1,260 square feet (45–115 square m). The pit-house roof was usually conical and was supported by a framework of wooden posts, beams, and stringers—long saplings that had been stripped of bark and were used to bridge the area between the beams or from the beams to the ground. The smoke hole in the top was also the entrance to the house. The interior was reached by climbing onto the roof, through the smoke hole, and down a ladder or notched log.

Once common throughout the Plateau region, pit houses were eventually supplanted in the southern Plateau by the mat-covered surface house. These homes used a conical or A-frame design that was formed by leaning together stringers or timbers and covering them with mats made of tule, a type of reed. As the availability of

TEPEES

Conical tents, or tepees (tipis), were most common to the North American Plains Indians. Although a number of Native American groups used similar structures during the hunting season, only the Plains Indians adopted tepees as year-round dwellings, and then only from the 17th century onward. At that time the Spanish introduction of horses, guns, and metal implements enabled Plains peoples to become mounted nomads. The tepee was an ideal dwelling for these groups, as it could be easily disassembled and transported.

The tepee was generally made by stretching a cover sewn of dressed buffalo skins over a framework of wooden poles. In some cases reed mats, canvas, sheets of bark, or other materials were used for the covering. Women were responsible for tepee construction and maintenance. In raising a tepee, a woman would begin with 3 or 4 poles, depending upon her tribe's preferences. These first few poles acted as the keystones of a conical

Three Native American men on the shore of the Columbia River stand next to their tepees, c. 1922. Library of Congress Prints and Photographs Division

framework that was augmented by some 20 to 30 lighter poles, all leaning toward a central point and tied together a short distance from the top. An adjustable flap was left open at the top to allow smoke to escape, and a flap at the bottom served as a doorway. Tepees were usually 12 to 20 feet (3.5 to 6 m) high and 15 to 30 feet (4.5 to 9 m) in diameter, although larger structures were not uncommon. When very large shelters were needed, two pole frameworks could be set adjacent to one another in a figure-eight shape, with poles and covers left out of the adjoining walls. Many examples are known of small tepees sized for children's playhouses and very small tepees sized for dollhouses.

It was common for Native Americans to devote much of the winter season to decorating their tepees with colourful paintings of animals and the hunt. The beauty and gracefulness of the tepee made it the popular image of the home of all indigenous Americans, although the wickiup (wigwam), hogan, igloo, longhouse, pueblo, and earth lodge were equally important examples of Native American dwellings.

Euro-American goods increased, Plateau peoples often covered surface houses with canvas rather than reed mats, which were time-consuming to produce.

Conical houses had one hearth in the centre of the floor and generally sheltered one nuclear or three-generation family. These tepeelike, lightly built structures were used in summer when families were engaged in nomadic foraging activities. They averaged perhaps 15 to 30 feet (4.5 to 9 m) in diameter, with an interior space of approximately 175–700 square feet (16–65 sq m). In contrast, A-frame houses were used as communal winter residences, so they were very large, heavily built, and thoroughly insulated. Early visitors to the Plateau report houses as long as 150 feet (45 m). More typical were houses between 25 and 60 feet (7.5 and 18 m) long and perhaps 12 to 15 feet (3.5 to 4.5 m) wide, for an interior of approximately 300–900 square feet (28–85 sq m). Hearths were placed at intervals down the central aisle and were usually shared by two nuclear families, one on each side of the aisle.

The shelters used at foraging camps could take a variety of forms, ranging from small conical mat lodges to simple windbreaks. Groups that traveled to the Plains to hunt bison typically used the tepee during those expeditions. As they became increasingly nomadic, many of these groups adopted the tepee as a full-time dwelling, like the Plains peoples.

FOOD AND TRANSPORTATION

The peoples of the Plateau were hunter-gatherers, relying on wild foods for subsistence. Salmon, trout, eels, suckers, and other fish were abundant in the rivers, and fishing was the most important source of food. Among the tools they used for fishing were one- or three-pronged fish spears, traps, and nets. Communities also built and held in common large fish weirs—stone or wooden enclosures used to "corral" the catch. Substantial quantities of fish were dried on elevated wooden racks and preserved for winter consumption. The region's fauna included deer, elk, bear, caribou, and small game. Hunters used a bow and arrows and sometimes a short spear in their pursuit of such prey. In the winter they wore long and narrow snowshoes to facilitate the tracking of animals.

Among the wild plant foods that were obtained, roots and bulbs were especially important. The major source of starch was the bulb of the camas flower (*Camassia esculenta*). Bitterroot, onions, wild carrots, and parsnips were also gathered and were generally cooked in earth ovens heated by hot stones. Berries—serviceberries, huckleberries, blueberries, and others—were harvested as well.

The earliest European explorers in the region reported that Plateau clothing comprised a bark breechcloth or apron and a twined bark poncho that fell a little below the waist. During the cold season men wrapped their legs with fur, women had leggings of hemp, and robes or blankets of rabbit or other fur were used. By the 19th century, however, clothing had become similar to that seen on the Plains: men wore breechcloths, leggings, and shirts, and women wore leggings and dresses. Hair was generally braided, and hats, headbands, feathered battle and ceremonial regalia, and other headgear had also become common.

The Chinook, who traded in slaves, molded the heads of freeborn infants with a device attached to the cradleboard. Despite their name, the Flathead did not engage in this form of modification. Some early ethnographers speculated that the apparent misnomer derived from the group's squareness of profile relative to the triangular form seen in skulls that had been altered. Many historic paintings that purport to depict Flathead individuals are actually portraits of members of neighbouring tribes.

Dugout or bark canoes were useful forms of transportation, although long-distance water travel was limited by the many river rapids in the region. Items that were small or could be manufactured by one or two people were typically the property of individuals. Groups whose territory adjoined that of the Northwest Coast Indians engaged in a variety of redistributive events similar to potlatches. Decorative art consisted of pictographic designs with a symbolic content, referring to supernatural beings and cosmic things.

The general ethos emphasized material equality and the sharing of necessities. Food resources, for instance, were generally shared. The Klamath, however, held wealthy persons in greater esteem than others, an ethos that may have derived from the tribe's proximity to the hierarchical societies of the Northwest Coast and California.

AUTHORITY

The key sociopolitical unit in traditional Plateau societies was the village, but the means of governing each village varied from tribe to tribe. The Ntlakapamux, for example, used a fairly informal consensus system. The Sanpoil, on the other hand, had a more formal political structure: the village had a chief, a subchief, and a general assembly in which every adult had a vote—except for young men who were not married. The Flathead were perhaps the most hierarchical group, with a head chief of great power and band chiefs under him. The head chief decided on matters of peace and war and was not bound by the recommendations of his council.

Chiefs and their families usually played a prominent role in promoting traditional values. Among the Sinkaietk, for instance, chiefly office was hereditary. While conferring a level of decision-making power, the office also obligated the chief and his family to act in ways that exemplified virtuous behaviour. For this group such behaviour included the placement of a female relative among the chief's advisers. Similar positions for highly respected women also existed in other groups, such as the Coeur d'Alene, and bear witness to the independence of women in many Plateau tribes.

Force was rarely used as a means of social control. Instead, social pressure and public opinion were employed. People were not coerced into following the advice of a chief or the decisions of a council meeting. Those who did not agree with a given course of action could simply move to another village or another band and did so fairly frequently. However, a number of groups allowed chiefs, village councils, or a combination thereof to arbitrate or punish transgressions against the community such as murder or stealing. Arbitrations generally involved a settlement of horses to the injured party, while corporal punishment was usually administered by a delegated village "whipper." Slaves were compelled to follow their owners' wishes.

In some cases, as with the Nez Percé's transition from settled village life to a more nomadic existence, political organization was adjusted. The Nez Percé were originally a village-centred people. Each village had a male chief whose office was hereditary, although poorly qualified sons were generally passed over for the privilege. The chief was advised by a council and was primarily occupied with mediating disputes, displaying exemplary behaviour, and seeing to the general good of his people. By the early 19th century, however, families from different villages had begun to coalesce into mobile bands in order to undertake autumn hunts on the Plains. While the hereditary authority of the village chiefs continued, leadership in the new tasks associated with this change in lifestyle—notably travel, defense, and raiding—came under the authority of skilled hunters and fighters.

KINSHIP

Most Plateau peoples followed what anthropologists call a bilateral descent system. In these systems descent is traced equally through the lines of the mother and the father. The nuclear family and its closest relatives constituted the average Plateau kin groups. This was the case among, for instance, the Tenino. Their kinship terminology revealed the close connection between family relatives of the same generation, so that all one's female cousins were called by and treated in the same terms as those used for one's sisters. One's male cousins, likewise, were all one's "brothers."

Marriage and divorce were informal affairs. (That said, as first cousins were essentially considered siblings, they did not marry.) Newlyweds generally resided near the groom's family, and in case of divorce the wife simply returned to her parents' home. No particular grounds for separation were necessary, and at a later date both parties usually undertook new marriages. Polygyny, a form of marriage in which several wives share a husband, was an approved but not especially common practice throughout the culture area.

Some Plateau kinship systems included "joking relationships," informal mechanisms for expressing social disapproval or deflating puffed egos.

RITES OF PASSAGE

Human life in all societies was—and still is—marked by fixed ritual acts that open the gateway to the different social roles one has to perform. For the Plateau peoples, these rituals began before birth. Among the Sinkaietk, for example, a pregnant woman was expected to give birth in a lodge that had been constructed for this purpose. A newborn spent its day strapped in a cradleboard. Naming practices varied among the tribes. The training of the child was left to the mother and grandmother, but even young Sinkaietk boys could accompany their fathers on fishing and small-game hunting trips, while young girls helped their mothers about the house and in gathering wild foods. Children learned to be hardy through activities such as swimming in cold streams. Such exertions were generally supervised by grandparents. Disobedience was rare. When it did occur, it was sometimes met with

JOKING RELATIONSHIPS

Anthropologists call the relationship between two individuals or groups that allows or requires unusually free verbal or physical interaction a joking relationship. The interaction may be mutual (symmetrical) or formalized in such a way that one person or group does the teasing and the other is not allowed to retaliate (asymmetrical). The type of interaction varies and may include light teasing, chastisement, verbal abuse, sexual ribaldry, or horseplay.

Joking relationships generally occur in one of three forms, all of which are generally found in situations in which conflict or rivalry is possible but must be avoided. In one form, it is used as an instrument of social sanction, with the joker calling public attention to an individual or a group that has behaved in a socially unacceptable way. When such a relationship obtains between groups, the jocularity or critique, although disrespectful, expresses the separateness of the groups in a manner that averts actual conflict.

The second form of joking relationship is often found in association with the avoidance relationship, which limits direct personal contact and maintains an extreme degree of respect between categories of people. In such cases, joking relationships are typically prescribed between people of opposite sex who are potential partners in marriage or sexual relations, while avoidance relations are required between persons of opposite sex for whom marital or sexual relations are forbidden. Both of these customs—viewed as points along a continuum of respectful behaviour ranging from avoidance to license—act to stabilize relations that might be subject to conflict. For example, in many cultures a man must avoid his mother-in-law and joke with his sisters-in-law, while a woman must avoid her father-in-law and joke with her brothers-in-law.

The third common form of joking relationship occurs between people of alternating generations. In these cases, grandparents and grandchildren share an especially fond relationship that is characterized by interactions ranging from gentle teasing to explicit or coarse descriptions of one another's body parts or bodily functions. In contrast, relationships between parents and children tend to be more formal and oriented toward discipline. As with the other forms, this kind of joking relationship separates people into those from whom one may expect social support and those from whom one may expect social sanction.

Among the Plains Indians, some joking relationships were quite ribald. Many of the tribes adhering strictly to the avoidance taboo that pertained largely to in-laws permitted great freedom between a man and his sisters-in-law. Among the Crow they were expected to interact with each other and to talk to each other in vile or sexually explicit language. The Atsina encouraged mutual practical joking and teasing, and the Blackfoot allowed the same freedom as between husband and wife. It is notable that, according to marriage rules on the Plains, the parties to these joking relationships were potential mates.

corporal punishment. Some groups allowed parents to call upon the village whipper when children misbehaved.

Upon entering puberty a boy would undertake a vision quest, a rite of passage that usually involved spending some days fasting on a mountaintop in hopes of communicating with a guardian spirit. A girl who had her first menstruation was taken to a location some distance from the village and provided with living quarters. During this time she was seen as extremely powerful in the spiritual and supernatural senses and so observed a number of ritual taboos that were meant to protect her and the community. Among other actions, her hair was bound up in rolls that she touched only with a small comb, her face was painted red or yellow, she wore undecorated clothing, and she used a drinking tube rather than taking water directly from a well. After the flow, she ritually purified herself in a sweat lodge. Her seclusion might continue for one or several

HEAD FLATTENING

The practice of intentionally changing the shape of the human skull was once common in some cultures. Head flattening was practiced by a number of North, Central, and South American Indian tribes, particularly before European colonization. In fact, cases of cranial modification are known from all continents except Australia and Oceania, although it was rather rare in Africa south of the Sahara and apparently absent from South India.

The practice was most commonly accomplished by securing an infant in a cradleboard that had a moveable cover over the forehead. The pressure of the cover, gently and consistently applied over time, caused the child's forehead to elongate, creating a nearly smooth silhouette from the tip of the nose to the crown of the head. Flattening could also be achieved by binding an infant's head with cloth. Head flattening appears to have had no effect on an individual's mental capabilities.

months, during which time she might undertake a vision quest. She finished her seclusion with evening prayers on a hill. When she returned to the village, she was treated as an adult.

When an individual died, the living were expected to perform certain rituals. To prevent the dead from lingering among them, some groups demolished homes where death had occurred. Grave sites were often located at riversides, though the specific form of burial—whether the body was intact or cremated, placed on the surface or in the ground, covered with soil or a rock slide, and marked with stones or wood—varied from one tribe to another. For about one year after the death, the decedent's spouse (or spouses, in polygynous marriages) was expected to demonstrate grief by wearing old or ragged clothing and was also expected to delay remarriage during this period.

RELIGION

Religious beliefs, like the rest of the culture, were closely intertwined with the region's ecology. Animism, shamanism, and individual communion with the spirit world were religious practices that the Plateau Indians shared with indigenous North American religions in general.

Principal rituals consisted of the vision quest, which was compulsory for boys and recommended for girls; the firstling, or first foods, rites; and the winter dance. The first of these, the vision quest, was a means of engaging with the spirit-beings thought to guide individuals to particular vocations, such as hunting, warfare, or healing. Both boys and girls could become shamans, though it was seen as a more suitable occupation for the former. Shamans were believed to cure diseases by extracting a bad spirit or an object that had entered the sufferer's body. On the northern Plateau another shamanic role was to return souls that had been stolen by the dead, and shamans were known to publicize their feats through dramatic pantomimes. Because their work included healing the living and contacting the dead, shamans tended to be both wealthy and respected—and even feared.

Firstling rites celebrated and honoured the first foods that were caught or gathered in the spring. The first salmon ceremony celebrated the arrival of the salmon run. The first fish caught was ritually sliced, small pieces of it were distributed among the people and eaten, and the carcass was returned to the water accompanied by prayers and thanks. This ritual ensured that the salmon would return and have a good run the next year. Some Salish had a "salmon chief" who organized the ritual. The Okanagan, Ntlakapamux, and Lillooet celebrated similar rites for the first berries rather than the first salmon.

The winter or spirit dance was a ceremonial meeting at which participants personified their respective guardian spirits. Among the Nez Percé the dramatic performances and the songs were thought to bring warm weather, plentiful game, and successful hunts.

As in much of Northern America, folklore in the Plateau generally emphasized the creator, trickster, and culture hero Coyote. The subject of innumerable trickster tales, Coyote (or alternative trickster figures such as Bluejay) undertook exploits that reflected common foibles and reinforced the social mores of the people.

Chapter 2

CULTURAL CHANGE AMONG THE PLATEAU INDIANS

The most dynamic period of cultural change for the Plateau peoples occurred after the arrival of the horse in the early 18th century. Horse technology inspired innovations in all areas of traditional Plateau life, especially subsistence, political organization, and housing. It could also displace people: pressure from the nomadic Blackfoot in approximately 1800 forced the Flathead and Kutenai to withdraw from their home quarters on the plains of western Montana. They resettled in the intermontane valleys of the Rockies and from there made occasional buffalo hunts on the Plains in the company of other Plateau tribes such as the Coeur d'Alene and Nez Percé.

THE 19TH CENTURY

Plateau life changed in other ways, as well, notably by interaction with white travellers, traders, missionaries, and settlers. Direct contact between indigenous groups and Euro-Americans were relatively brief at first and included the provision of boats and food to the Lewis and Clark Expedition, which traversed the region in 1805 and again in 1806. Early in the 19th century the fur trade brought Native American and Euro-American trappers from the east into the country, particularly to the northern Plateau. These groups included a relatively large number of Iroquois men who had adopted Roman Catholicism. They propagated Christianity among the Flathead, who thereafter visited St. Louis to call on missionaries. Proselytizing missionaries were a strong force in the area from the 1820s to the '50s.

SYNCRETISM

By the 1830s many Plateau peoples were engaging in syn-cretic (blended) religious practices through millenarian movements, which are characterized by the belief that the end of the world is imminent and that a new heaven or new earth will replace the old one. The practices came to be known collectively as the Prophet Dance. The major impetus for that movement appears to have been despair over the devastating loss of life caused by the epidemic dis-eases that had accompanied European colonization. The eponymous prophets were charismatic leaders who were said to have received supernatural instructions for hasten-ing the renewal of the world and the return of the dead. The Prophet Dance movement appeared before that of the Ghost Dance. Like the Ghost Dance, variations on the Prophet Dance persisted into the 21st century.

DISENFRANCHISEMENT

By the 1840s the homestead movement was flourishing. Thousands of emigrants were inspired to move to the Willamette valley and other parts of what would become the Oregon Territory. Many of these settlers traveled through the Plateau, often trespassing on tribal lands. Native peoples also noted with consternation that dis-ease seemed to follow the Euro-American missionaries and settlers. Conflict ensued, and by the 1850s the United States had begun to negotiate treaties with the resident tribes. For the most part these involved setting terms for regional development and delineating specific tracts of

PROPHET DANCE AND GHOST DANCE

The Plateau Indians of the early 19th century practiced a ritual during which the participants danced in order to hasten the return of the dead and the renewal of the world, particularly as it had been before European contact. This ritual, known as the Prophet Dance, was a precursor of the Ghost Dance movement of the 1870s and a later incarnation in the 1890s. Both the Prophet Dance and the Ghost Dance movement represented an attempt of Indians in the western United States to rehabilitate their traditional cultures.

Both Ghost Dance cults arose from Northern Paiute prophet-dreamers in western Nevada who announced the imminent return of the dead (hence "ghost"), the ousting of the whites, and the restoration of Indian lands, food supplies, and way of life. These ends, it was believed, would be hastened by the dances and songs revealed to the prophets in their vision visits

Ghost Dance of the Sioux, *print from a wood engraving, 1891.*
Library of Congress Prints and Photographs Division

to the spirit world and also by strict observance of a moral code that resembled Christian teaching and forbade war of any sort. Many dancers fell into trances and received new songs from the dead they met in visions or were healed by Ghost Dance rituals.

The first Ghost Dance developed in 1869 around the shaman and dreamer Wodziwob (d. *c.* 1872) and in 1871–73 spread to California and Oregon tribes. It soon died out or was transformed into other cults. The second movement derived from Wovoka (*c.* 1856–1932), whose father, Tavibo, had assisted Wodziwob. Wovoka had been influenced by Presbyterians on whose ranch he worked, by Mormons, and by the Indian Shaker Church. During a solar eclipse in January 1889, he had a vision of dying, speaking with God in heaven, and being commissioned to teach the new dance and millennial message. Indians from many tribes traveled to learn from Wovoka, whose self-inflicted stigmata on hands and feet encouraged belief in him as a new messiah, or Jesus Christ, come to the Indians.

Thus, the Ghost Dance spread as far as the Missouri River, the Canadian border, the Sierra Nevada, and northern Texas. Early in 1890 it reached the Sioux, who—reaching out for some hope of salvation from hard conditions, such as semistarvation caused by reduction in the size of their reservation in the late 1880s—responded affirmatively to Wovoka. The Ghost Dance caused alarm among whites and led to federal military intervention. The army subdued the Ghost Dance movement, but the movement was wrongly blamed for the Sioux outbreak (actually a response to the killing of Chief Sitting Bull during his arrest) that culminated in the massacre at Wounded Knee Creek. Of the few hundred Sioux who left their reservation at Pine Ridge, seeking to hide in the Badlands—a barren region covering some 2,000 sq mi (5,200 square km) of southwestern South Dakota— more than 140, including women and children, were killed in the incident now known as the Wounded Knee massacre.

land as belonging to either the tribes or the government. The treaty process was disrupted in 1857, before completion, when the discovery of gold on the Thompson River spurred a great influx of settlers and miners. Gold strikes were soon found on several other rivers in the region. Tensions rose; crowded mining camps bred infectious diseases, and the men drawn to such enterprises were often corrupt and predatory.

The turbulence of the rest of the century left many Plateau tribes struggling economically. The United States and Canada invoked a series of public policies to assimilate indigenous peoples: tribes were confined to reservations, subsistence practices were forcibly shifted from hunting and gathering to agriculture, and children were sent to boarding schools where they were often physically abused. The region was also affected by placer mining, a technique in which water from high-pressure hoses is used to strip soil from hillsides into rivers. This greatly increased the sediment load of waterways and depleted crucial salmon stocks. Fisheries were further decimated by industrial harvesting at the mouths of the great rivers. Used to supply a burgeoning cannery industry, the new techniques not only caught enormous quantities of fish but did so before the salmon could reach their spawning grounds and reproduce.

As subsistence became increasingly difficult, some indigenous groups became more resistant to government policies. In the early 1870s a band of Modoc, dissatisfied with farming life and the suppression of their religious practices, left their assigned reservation and returned to their original land near Tule Lake. The Modoc War (1872–73) comprised the federal government's attempt to return this band to the reservation. Unable to apprehend the group, the military finally used siege tactics to force its surrender.

The Nez Percé War of 1877 resulted from two otherwise unrelated events: a shady treaty negotiation that ceded some tribal lands and a raid in the Wallowa valley in which several settlers were killed. Following the raid, the United States ordered all bands of Nez Percé off of the

The son of a Nez Percé mother and a Scottish father, Nez Percé tribesman Duncan McDonald is seen here with his wife Quilsuh sometime around the turn of the 20th century in Montana. McDonald wrote historical accounts in English from a Native American perspective, notably of the Nez Percé War of 1877. Transcendental Graphics/Archive Photos/Getty Images

relinquished lands, including the Wallowa valley. The band that had remained resident there was led by Nez Percé Chief Joseph and comprised more than 500 individuals, many of them women, children, or elders. Fearing disproportionate reprisals from the military, the band fled. The group was eventually captured, but only after a chase of

SMOHALLA

(b. c. 1815 or 1820, Upper Columbia River, Oregon Country [United States]—d. 1895, Satus Creek, Yakama Reservation)

The prophet, preacher, and teacher Smohalla was one of a series of leaders who arose in response to the menace presented to Indian life and culture by the encroachment of white settlers. He founded a religious cult, the Dreamers, that emphasized traditional Indian values.

The name Smohalla—which means "Dreamer"—is also given as Smowholla, Shmoqula, and Smuxale. He belonged to the Wanapum, a small Sahaptin-speaking tribe closely related to the Nez Percé and centring on the Priest Rapids area of the Columbia River in what is now eastern Washington State. He grew up to become a locally celebrated medicine man and a warrior of distinction. After a fight with a rival, he left his home and went south, traveling perhaps as far as Mexico, and was away for several years. When he returned, he announced that he had died and been resurrected by God. He began to preach, becoming known to his own people as Yuyunipitquana ("Shouting Mountain"), and by 1872 he had a large following.

White settlers had been coming into the Northwest in large numbers, and the completion of the Northern Pacific Railway increased the flow. The U.S. government was trying to persuade the Indians to move to reservations or to take up homesteads and become farmers. The Plateau Indians had been largely fishermen and hunters, but many of them accepted the government's proposals and turned to agriculture. Smohalla taught that the Indians alone were real people, the first created, and that whites, blacks, and Chinese had been created later by God to punish the Indians for leaving their ancient ways. They must live as their fathers had done, and, above all, not plow land (i.e., wound Mother Earth) or sign papers for land, which was against nature.

If they lived as their fathers had and followed the ritual of Smohalla's Dreamer cult, they would be aided by the forces of nature, as well as by hordes of Indian dead, who would be resurrected. God would drive away the non-Indians. The Dreamers got their name from the emphasis Smohalla placed on dreams sent to himself and his priests by God to direct them in the right ways. The ritual emphasized drumming, ringing of bells, and ecstatic dancing, all of which combined to bring on visions and exaltation.

Smohalla's influence spread among the Plateau Indians, Chief Joseph and the Nez Percé being among his most devoted followers. The cult was for a generation the greatest barrier to the U.S. government's efforts to settle the Indians of the region and to assimilate them, and it persisted for several years after Smohalla's death.

more than three months during which the people traveled some 1,600–1,700 miles (2,575–2,700 km).

In the 1880s, in a process known as "allotment," the common title to land that had been conferred to each tribe was replaced with individual titles to farm-sized acreages. The remainder was then sold, severely reducing indigenous landholdings in the Plateau. Although legal safeguards were put into place to protect indigenous landowners from exploitation and corruption, such laws were poorly enforced. As a result, allotment initiated a period of increasing poverty for many Plateau tribes.

THE 20TH CENTURY AND BEYOND: THE STRUGGLE FOR SOVEREIGNTY

Following decades of paternalism, the U.S. Bureau of Indian Affairs in the 1930s revisited its policies and gave

INDIAN GAMING

Although Native Americans have developed a variety of businesses, the most important tool of economic development for many U.S. tribes has been the gaming industry. The term *Indian gaming* refers to the gambling enterprises that are owned by federally recognized Native American tribal governments and that operate on reservation or other tribal lands. Indian gaming includes a range of business operations, from full casino facilities with slot machines and Las Vegas-style high-stakes gambling to smaller facilities offering games such as bingo, lotteries, and video poker. Because U.S. laws recognize certain forms of tribal sovereignty and self-government, native-owned casinos enjoy some immunity from direct regulation by individual states. However, tribal gaming operations must comply with the Indian Gaming Regulatory Act of 1988 and other federal laws.

The first Indian casino was built in Florida by the Seminole tribe, which opened a successful high-stakes bingo parlour in 1979. Other indigenous nations quickly followed suit, and by 2000 more than 150 tribes in 24 states had opened casino or bingo operations on their reservations.

INDIAN GAMING STATES

States with casino gambling operations

© 2008 Encyclopædia Britannica, Inc.

U.S. states that allow Indian gaming.

The first years of the 21st century saw precipitous growth: by 2005, annual revenues had reached more than $22 billion, and Indian gaming accounted for about 25 percent of all legal gambling receipts in the United States. This was about the same amount generated by the country's aggregate state lotteries, albeit somewhat less than the 40 percent share generated by commercial casinos in Nevada, Florida, and New Jersey. Notably—and unlike gambling operations run by non-Indians—tribal casinos are required by law to contribute a percentage of their annual revenue to state-controlled trust funds. These funds are then distributed to local communities to offset costs related to the subsidiary effects of tribal gaming operations, such as the expansion or maintenance of transportation, electrical, or sewage systems and other forms of infrastructure; the need for increased traffic patrols; and treatment for gambling addiction. Some of these funds are also distributed as assistance to tribes that do not have gaming operations.

The prosperity of Indian gaming operations depends to a great extent on location. Those near or in major urban areas can be very successful, while those in remote areas (where many reservations are located) tend to generate much less revenue. Although tribes with successful operations have been able to use gaming income to improve the general health, education, and cultural well-being of their members, many Indian casinos have not made significant profits. Thus, the success of some operations on some reservations cannot be generalized to all casinos or all reservations. To the contrary, U.S. census data consistently indicate that the legalization of Indian gaming has not affected the indigenous population in aggregate: Native Americans remain the most impoverished and underprivileged minority community in the United States.

Indian gaming has been at the centre of political controversy since the late 1970s. In many cases the debate has revolved around the morality or immorality of gambling; this issue, of course, is not unique to Indian gaming in particular. Controversies involving Indian gaming operations per se have generally focused instead on whether the unique legal status of tribes, which allows them the privilege of owning and operating such businesses, should be retained or discontinued; whether Indians have sufficient acumen or training to run such businesses; whether engaging in entrepreneurial capitalism inherently undercuts indigenous ethnic identities; and whether gaming is a desirable addition to a specific local economy.

self-governing power to tribes, authorizing them to create governments and corporations. Further, tribes were put in charge of other aspects of community life, such as the administration of schools. Many tribes chartered constitutions or similar documents, elected councils, and engaged in other forms of self-governance during this period.

In 1954 the federal government terminated its relationship with the inhabitants of the Modoc and Klamath

Indian-run casinos, such as this one in Minnesota, became an important source of income for some Native American peoples in the late 20th and early 21st centuries. Antonio Ribeiro/Gamma-Rapho/Getty Images

reservation, stripping the tribe of federal recognition and the benefits and protections associated with that status. Termination was a national policy. Its hope was that the elimination of the special relationship between the federal government and indigenous peoples would encourage economic development on reservations. The reservation land that had survived allotment was condemned and sold, with the proceeds distributed among the former residents. The loss of federal support for health care and schools devastated the community. The Modoc and Klamath people sued to regain federal recognition, which they achieved in 1986, but they did not regain their former lands.

As the 20th century progressed, many tribes sued the governments of Canada and the United States in order to reclaim territory, generally claiming illegal takings due to treaty violations or unconscionably low compensation. A number of these suits were successful and resulted in awards in the tens of millions of dollars. Most of the monetary awards were distributed among all members of a tribe rather than held as common assets, however, and so were not available for reservationwide improvements. Treaty-ensured fishing rights were also the substance of legal action, especially after major dam construction on the Columbia and other rivers abrogated those rights by destroying traditional fishing sites. Again, the tribes were generally successful in gaining compensation for their losses.

In the late 20th and early 21st centuries, many Plateau tribes had regrouped from the economic devastation of the previous 100 years or more. Several had added tourist resorts and casinos to their extant timber, ranching, and fishing operations. Funds from these enterprises were used for a variety of community purposes, including education, health care, rural development, and cultural preservation.

Chapter 3
SELECTED PLATEAU PEOPLES IN FOCUS

As mentioned previously, there are four main languages families in the Plateau culture area. These are Salishan (Salish), represented here by the Flathead peoples; Sahaptin, here represented by Nez Percé and the Yakama; Kutenai, a language isolate (that is, a language unrelated to the other languages of the region); and Klamath-Modoc, two very similar dialects spoken by the Klamath and Modoc peoples that may be related to Sahaptin.

FLATHEAD (SALISHAN)

The Flathead are a tribe of what is now western Montana, U.S., whose original territory extended from the crest of the Bitterroot Range to the Continental Divide of the Rocky Mountains and centred on the upper reaches of the Clark Fork of the Columbia River. Although early accounts referred to all Salish-speaking tribes as "Flathead," the people now known by this name never actually engaged in head flattening.

As was the case with other tribes that regularly crossed the Rocky Mountains, the Flathead—the easternmost of the Plateau Indians—shared many traits with nomadic Plains Indians. They acquired horses in great numbers and mounted annual fall expeditions to hunt bison on the Plains, often warring with tribes that were permanent residents of the area. Traditional Flathead culture also emphasized Plains-type warfare and its honours, including staging war dances, killing enemies, kidnapping women and children, and stealing horses. Glory was also

Chief Charlot of the Flathead, photograph by Norman A. Forsyth, c. *1908.* Library of Congress, Washington, D.C. (neg. no. LC-USZ62-112331)

gained by an act known as "counting coup"—striking or touching an enemy in battle—which was generally considered of greater moment than killing him.

Before colonization, the Flathead usually lived in tepees. The A-framed mat-covered lodge, a typical Plateau structure, was also used. Western Flathead groups had bark canoes, while eastern groups used the bison-skin tubs known as bullboats that were typical of the Plains. Fishing was important among the Flathead, as it was among other Plateau tribes.

Traditional Flathead religion centred on guardian spirits, with whom individuals communicated in visions. A spirit could bring good fortune and health to the person it guarded or disease and misfortune to others. Shamanism was also important to traditional religious and healing practices.

In the 21st century, most individuals of this tribe referred to themselves simply as Salish, though in common parlance the name Salish refers to a much larger collection of tribes. Early 21st-century population estimates indicated more than 4,000 Flathead descendants. Most live on the Flathead Reservation (formally the Confederated Salish and Kootenai Tribes of the Flathead Reservation) in Lake County, Montana, the fourth-largest reservation within the United States.

SAHAPTIN

The Sahaptin (also Shahaptin, or Sahaptian) languages are classified within the Penutian family. The speakers of these languages traditionally resided in what are now southeastern Washington, northeastern Oregon, and west-central Idaho, U.S., in the basin of the Columbia River and its tributaries. Major groups included the Cayuse, Molala, Palouse (or Palus), Nez Percé, Tenino, Umatilla, Walla Walla, and Yakama (formerly spelled Yakima).

Nez Percé

Centring on the lower Snake River and such tributaries as the Salmon and Clearwater rivers in what is now northeastern Oregon, southeastern Washington, and central Idaho, U.S., the Nez Percé were the largest, most powerful, and best-known of the Sahaptin-speaking peoples. They were called by various names by other groups. The French name by which they are best known, Nez Percé ("Pierced Nose"), referred to the wearing of nose pendants, though the

Nez Percé man, c. 1905. Library of Congress Prints and Photographs Division

fashion does not seem to have been widespread among them. Their self-name is Nimi'ipuu.

Though considered to be Plateau Indians, as one of the Plateau's easternmost groups, the Nez Percé were influenced by the Plains Indians just east of the Rockies. Typical of the Plateau, Nez Percé domestic life traditionally centred on small villages located on streams having abundant salmon, which, dried, formed their main source of food. They also sought a variety of game, berries, and roots. Their dwellings were communal lodges—A-framed and covered with tule mats—varying in size and sometimes housing as many as 30 families.

After they acquired horses early in the 18th century, life for the Nez Percé began to change dramatically, at least among some groups. Horse transport enabled them to mount expeditions to the eastern slope of the Rockies, where they hunted bison and traded with Plains peoples. Always somewhat warlike, the Nez Percé became even more so, adopting many war honours, war dances, and battle tactics common to the Plains, as well as other forms of equestrian material culture such as the tepee. The Nez Percé built up one of the largest horse herds on the continent. They were almost unique among Native Americans in conducting a selective breeding program, and they were instrumental in creating the Appaloosa breed.

CHIEF JOSEPH

(b. c. 1840, Wallowa Valley, Oregon Territory—d. Sept. 21, 1904, Colville Reservation, Wash., U.S.),

The Nez Percé chief In-mut-too-yah-lat-lat (known as Chief Joseph), when faced with white settlement of tribal lands in Oregon, led his followers in a dramatic effort to escape to Canada.

The Nez Percé tribe was one of the most powerful in the Pacific Northwest and in the first half of the 19th century one of the most friendly to whites. Many Nez Percé, including Chief Joseph's father, were converted to Christianity and Chief Joseph was educated in a mission school. The advance of white settlers into the Pacific Northwest after 1850 caused the United States to press the Indians of the region to surrender their lands and accept resettlement on small and often unattractive reservations. Some Nez Percé chiefs, including Chief Joseph's father, questioned the validity of treaties pertaining to their lands negotiated in 1855 and 1863 on the ground that the chiefs who participated in the negotiations did not represent their tribe.

When the United States attempted in 1877 to force the dissenting Nez Percé to move to a reservation in Idaho, Chief Joseph, who had succeeded his father in 1871, reluctantly agreed. While he was preparing for the removal, however, he learned that a trio of young men had massacred a band of white settlers and prospectors. Fearing retaliation by the U.S. army, he decided instead to lead his small body of followers (some 200 to 300 warriors and their families) on a long trek to Canada.

For more than three months (June 17–Sept. 30, 1877), Chief Joseph led his followers on a retreat of about 1,600–1,700 miles (2,575–2,735 km) across Oregon, Washington, Idaho, and Montana, outmaneuvering the pursuing troops, which outnumbered Joseph's warriors by a ratio of at least ten to one, and several times defeating them in actual combat. During the long retreat, he won the admiration of many whites by his humane treatment of prisoners, his concern for women, children, and the aged, and also because he purchased supplies from ranchers and storekeepers rather than stealing them.

The Nez Percé were finally surrounded in the Bear Paw mountains of Montana, within 40 miles (64 km) of the Canadian border. On October 5 Chief Joseph surrendered to Gen. Nelson A. Miles, delivering an eloquent speech that was long remembered: "Hear me, my chiefs; my heart is sick and sad. From where the Sun now stands, I will fight no more forever."

Chief Joseph and his band were sent at first to a barren reservation in Indian Territory (later Oklahoma). There many sickened and died. Not until 1885 were he and the remnants of his tribe allowed to go to a reservation in Washington—though still in exile from their valley. Meanwhile, Chief Joseph had made two trips to Washington, D.C., where, presented to Pres. Theodore Roosevelt, he pleaded for the return of his people to their ancestral home.

As the 18th century progressed, the Nez Percé's increased mobility fostered their enrichment and expansionism, and they began to dominate negotiations with other tribes in the region. The 19th century was a period of increasing change in Nez Percé life. Just six years after the explorers Meriwether Lewis and William Clark visited the Nez Percé in 1805, fur traders and trappers began penetrating the area. They were followed later by missionaries. By the 1840s emigrant settlers were moving through the area on the Oregon Trail. In 1855 the Nez Percé agreed to a treaty with the United States that created a large reservation encompassing most of their traditional land. The 1860 discovery of gold on the Salmon and Clearwater rivers, which generated an influx of thousands of miners and settlers, led U.S. commissioners in 1863 to force renegotiation of the treaty. The new treaty reduced the size of the reservation by threefourths, and continued pressure from homesteaders and squatters reduced the area even more.

Many Nez Percé, perhaps a majority, had never accepted either treaty, and hostile actions and raids by both settlers and Native Americans eventually evolved into the Nez Percé War of 1877. For five months a small band of 250 Nez Percé warriors, under the leadership of Chief Joseph, held off a U.S. force of 5,000 troops led by Gen. O.O. Howard, who tracked them through Idaho, Yellowstone Park, and Montana before they surrendered to Gen. Nelson A. Miles. In the campaign, Chief Joseph lost 239 persons, including women and children, and the U.S. military lost 266. The tribe was then assigned to malarial country in Oklahoma rather than being returned to the Northwest as promised.

Early 21st-century population estimates indicated approximately 6,500 individuals of Nez Percé descent.

YAKAMA

The Yakama lived along the Columbia, Yakima, and Wenatchee rivers in what is now the south-central region of the state of Washington, U.S. As with many other Sahaptin-speaking Plateau Indians, they were primarily salmon fishers before colonization. In the 21st century the Yakama continued to be involved in wildlife management and fisheries.

The Yakama call themselves Waptailmim ("People of the Narrow River"). They acquired historical distinction in the Yakama Indian Wars (1855–58), an attempt by the tribe to resist U.S. forces intent upon clearing the Washington Territory for prospectors and settlers. The conflict stemmed from a treaty that had been negotiated in 1855, according to which the Yakama and 13 other tribes (identified in the treaty as Kah-milt-pah, Klikatat, Klinquit, Kow-was-say-ee, Li-ay-was, Oche-chotes, Palouse, Pisquouse, Se-ap-cat, Shyiks, Skin-pah, Wenatshapam, and Wish-ham) were to be placed on a reservation and confederated as the Yakama Nation. Before the treaty

Yakama man, c. 1910. Library of Congress Prints and Photographs Division

could be ratified, however, a force united under the leadership of Yakama chief Kamaiakan, who declared his intention to drive all nonnatives from the region. After initial Yakama successes, the uprising spread to other tribes in Washington and Oregon. Three years of raids, ambushes, and engagements followed, until September 1858, when the Native American forces were decisively defeated at the Battle of Four Lakes on a tributary of the Spokane River.

In 1859 the treaty of 1855 was effected, with the Yakama and most of the other tribes confined to reservations and their fertile ancestral lands opened to colonial appropriation. Since that time, all of the residents of the Yakama Reservation have been considered members of the Yakama Nation (Confederated Tribes and Bands of the Yakama Nation). Several tribes in the region, notably the Paloos (Palouse), refused to acknowledge the treaty of 1855 and would not enter the reservation.

Early 21st-century population estimates indicated some 11,000 individuals of Yakama Nation ancestry.

OTHER LANGUAGES

The two other languages of the Plateau Indians are Kutenai (Kootenay), a language isolate, and Klamath-Modoc, which may be distantly related to Sahaptin. The name Kutenai is ethnolinguistic—that is, the name for the language and the people is the same. Klamath-Modoc represents two distinct but very similar tribes.

KUTENAI

The Kutenai traditionally lived in what are now southeastern British Columbia, northern Idaho, and northwestern

Kutenai Indians in Idaho, c. 1900. The woman in the foreground, with her back to the camera, is wearing a cradleboard, a device used by many Native American women to carry infants. Apic/Hulton Archive/Getty Images

Montana. They are thought to be descended from an ancient Blackfoot group that migrated westward from the Great Plains to the drainage of the Kootenay River, a tributary of the upper Columbia. Plentiful streams and lakes, adequate rainfall, and abundant game and fish made this area the most favourable part of the plateau between the Rockies and the Pacific Coast Ranges.

Traits of both Plains and Plateau Indians are found in the Kutenai culture. After acquiring horses, they engaged in annual bison hunts beyond the Rockies and into the Plains. The advent of horse transport also increased the importance and frequency of military activities. Formalized war honours became a means of social advancement, and increasing numbers of war captives (women and children, mostly Blackfoot) made slavery, adoption, and intermarriage more common. The Kutenai dressed in clothing made of antelope, deer, or buffalo hide (breechcloths for men, tunics for women), lived in conical tepees, and painted their garments, tents, and bodies much in the manner of the Plains tribes. Like other Plateau peoples, however, they engaged in communal fishing, built great bark and dugout canoes, and acknowledged a supreme chief only when undertaking special expeditions.

Among the Kutenai there were no clans, classes, or secret societies. They were divided loosely into bands, each with a nominal leader and an informal council of elders. They deified the sun and, like most other indigenous North American peoples, practiced animism, the belief that a multitude of spirits pervades all things in nature. Shamanism also had considerable influence within Kutenai culture.

Early 21st-century population estimates indicated more than 5,000 individuals of Kutenai descent.

Klamath woman in front of dwelling, c. *1923*. Buyenlarge/Archive Photos/Getty Images

MODOC AND KLAMATH

The Modoc and the Klamath are two neighbouring tribes who lived in what are now south-central Oregon and northern California, spoke related languages (or dialects) that may be related to Sahaptin, and shared many cultural traits. Their traditional territory lay in the southern Cascade Range and was some 100 miles (160 km) long and 25 miles (40 km) wide, dotted with marshes, lakes, rivers, and streams. The Klamath, in the northern sectors, were primarily fishers and hunters of waterfowl. The Modoc, in the southern sectors, were also fishers but relied more on gathering edible roots, seeds, and berries and on hunting various game. Both tribes are considered to be Plateau Indians, though they were influenced by neighbouring

California Indians as well as those from the Northwest Coast and Great Basin.

The two tribes were organized into what were essentially autonomous villages; each had its own leaders, shamans, and medicine men. Although functioning independently in most situations, the villages would ally for war, and members of different villages often married. During winter, when snowdrifts could reach six feet (two metres) or more, most village families lived in semisubterranean earth-covered lodges, usually one family to a lodge. Poorer families lived in simpler mat-covered houses. In summer the usual dwelling was either a domed house of poles and matting or a lean-to of brush. Sweat houses, used by both men and women, doubled as community centres for prayer and other religious activities. Religious belief focused largely on guardian spirits, whose aid was sought for all manner of human accomplishments.

In 1864 the U.S. government pressed the two tribes to relinquish most of their territory and take up residence on a reservation around Upper Klamath Lake. The land was traditionally Klamath, however, and that tribe treated the Modoc as intruders. The U.S. government, moreover, failed in its treaty obligations to supply rations to the Modoc. Hence, in 1870 an insurgent band of Modocs under Kintpuash, a subchief known to the American military as Captain Jack, left the reservation. Federal efforts to induce this group's return precipitated the Modoc War of 1872–73, in which about 80 warriors and their families retreated to the California Lava Beds, a land of complex ravines and caves. There they mounted an effective resistance. After the murder of Brig. Gen. Edward Canby, who headed a peace commission in April 1873, U.S. troops prosecuted the war more vigorously. Betrayed by four of his followers, Captain Jack surrendered and was hanged. His followers were removed to Indian Territory (Oklahoma) and were not allowed to return to Oregon until 1909, after spending more than 30 years away from the region in which they sought to stay.

In the mid-20th century the U.S. government instituted a movement known as "termination," in which tribes lost federal recognition and the benefits and protections associated with that status. In 1954 the federal government terminated its relationship with the inhabitants of the Klamath reservation. The reservation land was condemned and sold, and the proceeds were distributed among the former residents. Most of the land was incorporated into the Winema National Forest. The Modoc and Klamath people regained federal recognition in 1986, but they did not regain their former reservation lands.

Population estimates indicated some 5,500 Modoc and Klamath descendants in the early 21st century.

Chapter 4

Traditional Culture of the Plains Indians

T he designation "Plains Indians" refers to any of the Native American peoples inhabiting the Great Plains of the United States and Canada. This culture area comprises a vast grassland that stretches from the Mississippi River to the Rocky Mountains and from the present-day provinces of Alberta, Saskatchewan, and Manitoba in Canada south to the present-day U.S. state of Texas. The area is drained principally by the Missouri and Mississippi rivers. The valleys of this watershed are the most reliable sites from which to obtain fresh water, wood, and most plant foods. The climate is continental, with annual temperatures ranging from below 0 °F (-18 °C) to as high as 110 °F (43 °C).

These peoples—perhaps because they were among the last indigenous peoples to be conquered in North America (some bands continued armed resistance into the 1880s)—are the archetypical American Indians of popular culture. Traveling exhibits such as artist George Catlin's Indian Gallery, "Wild West" shows such as that of William F. ("Buffalo Bill") Cody, and a multitude of toys, collectibles, pulp novels, films, television shows, and other consumer items supported this view.

LANGUAGES

The Plains culture area contained six distinct American Indian language families or stocks. While speakers of a language are generally referred to as a tribe or nation, this naming convention frequently conceals the presence of a

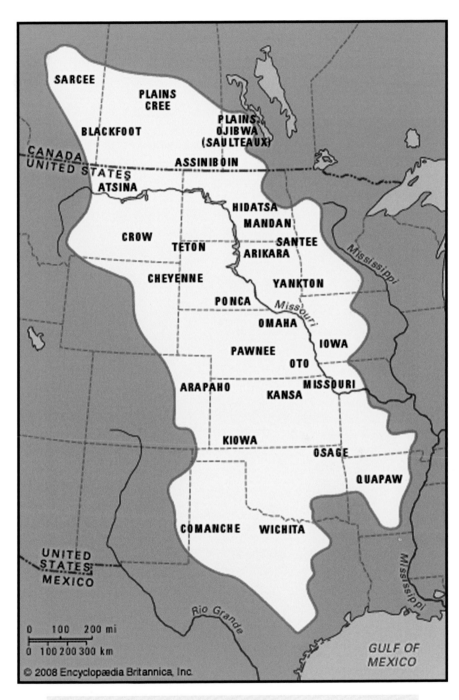

Distribution of North American Plains Indians.

GEORGE CATLIN

(b. July 26, 1796, Wilkes-Barre, Pa., U.S.—d. Dec. 23, 1872, Jersey City, N.J.)

The American artist and author George Catlin is noted for his paintings of Native American scenes, which constitute an invaluable record of Native American culture in the 19th century.

Catlin practiced law for a short time but in 1823 turned to portrait painting, in which he was self-taught. After achieving important commissions and critical acclaim, Catlin was elected to the National Academy of Design in 1826. He had been interested in Native American life from his boyhood, and in 1828, after encountering a delegation of Plains Indians in Philadelphia on their way to Washington, D.C., he became determined to record the Native American heritage before it was destroyed by the onslaught of the advancing American frontier. In 1830 he traveled west to St. Louis, and he began a series of visits to various tribes, chiefly in the Great Plains. He made more than 500 paintings and sketches based on his observations during

Comanche Village, Women Dressing Robes and Drying Meat, *oil on canvas, detail of a painting by George Catlin, 1834–35; in the Smithsonian American Art Museum, Washington, D.C.* Smithsonian American Art Museum/Art Resource, New York

his travels and exhibited these works in the United States and Europe from 1837 to 1845 as the "Indian Gallery." In 1841 he published his best-known book, the two-volume *Letters and Notes on the Manners, Customs, and Condition of the North American Indians*, which was illustrated with many engravings.

The bulk of Catlin's collection of works, which is mainly of ethnographic and historical interest, was acquired by the Smithsonian Institution in 1879. His other published works include *Catlin's North American Indian Portfolio: Hunting Scenes and Amusements of the Rocky Mountains and Prairies of America* (1845), *Catlin's Notes of Eight Years' Travels and Residence in Europe* (1848), *Life Amongst the Indians* (1867), and *Last Rambles Amongst the Indians of the Rocky Mountains and the Andes* (1867).

number of completely autonomous political divisions, or bands, within a given tribe. For instance, the Blackfoot tribe included three independent bands, the Piegan (also spelled Peigan), Blood (Kainah), and Northern Blackfoot (Siksika).

Each of the six language families was also represented by groups living in other culture areas, and the speakers of the several languages within a stock were not always geographically contiguous. Thus the speakers of Algonquian languages included the Blackfoot, Arapaho, Atsina, Plains Cree, and Saulteaux (Plains Ojibwa), all in the northern Plains, while Cheyenne, also an Algonquian language, was spoken in the central Plains.

The speakers of Siouan languages included the Mandan, Hidatsa, Crow, Assiniboin, Omaha, Ponca, Osage, Kansa, Iowa, Oto, and Missouri. Dakota, Lakota, and Nakota were spoken by the bands of the Santee, Teton, and Yankton Sioux tribes, respectively.

The Pawnee, Arikara, and Wichita were Caddoan-speakers, whereas the Wind River Shoshone and the

Comanche were of the Uto-Aztecan language family. The Athabaskan (Na-Dené) stock was represented by the Sarcee in the northern Plains, while the Kiowa-Tanoan stock was represented by the Kiowa.

Two other communication systems bear mention. The Métis of the Canadian Plains spoke Michif, a trade dialect that combined Plains Cree, an Algonquian language, and French. Michif was spoken over a wide area. In other areas many tribes used Plains Indian sign language as a means of communication.

THE ROLE OF THE HORSE IN PLAINS LIFE

So profound were the changes to material life on the Plains after the arrival of the horse that historians of the region often divide its history into two periods: pre- and post-horse. The change was a gradual one that took place over the course of at least a century. Before 1650 CE horses were fairly rare on the Plains, and by 1750 they had become relatively common. They greatly increased human mobility and productivity.

BEFORE THE HORSE

Going back at least 10,000 years ago until roughly 1100 CE, the Plains were very sparsely populated by humans. Plains residents, like hunting and gathering cultures worldwide, lived in small family-based groups, usually of no more than a few dozen individuals, and foraged widely over the landscape. The peoples of deep prehistory in this region are referred to as Paleo-Indians, Archaic cultures, and Plains Woodland cultures.

For some residents of the central Plains, circumstances had changed by approximately 850 CE. At that time a significant portion of their subsistence was provided by means of settled agriculture rather than from foraging. These farmers were living in settlements comprising a number of large earth-berm constructions (i.e., houses having earth piled against the exterior walls). As early as 1100, and no later than about 1250, most Plains residents had made this shift and were living in substantial villages and hamlets along the Missouri River and its tributaries. From north to south these groups eventually included the Hidatsa, Mandan, Arikara, Ponca, Omaha, Pawnee, Kansa, Osage, and Wichita. Some villages reached populations of up to a few thousand people. These groups, known as Plains Village cultures, grew maize (corn), beans, squash, and sunflowers in the easily tilled land along the river bottoms. Women were responsible for agricultural production and cultivated their crops using antler rakes, wooden digging sticks, and hoes made from the shoulder blades of elk or buffalo. Women also collected medicinal plants and wild produce such as prairie turnips and choke-cherries. Men grew tobacco and hunted bison, elk, deer, and other game. Whole communities would also participate in driving herds of big game over cliffs. Fish, fowl, and small game were also eaten.

Until the advent of the horse the only domesticated animals were dogs. These were mostly used as draft animals. Dogs drew the travois, a vehicle consisting of two poles in the shape of a V, with the open end of the V dragging on the ground. Burdens were placed on a platform that bridged the two poles. Because of the limitations inherent in using only dogs and people to carry loads, Plains peoples did not generally engage in extensive travel before the horse. However, Francisco Vázquez de Coronado's expedition in 1541 reported encounters with fully nomadic buffalo-hunting tribes on the southern Plains who had only dogs for transport.

Before horses became available, intertribal warfare was relatively rare and few battles were deadly. However, a period of exceptional conflict occurred in the 14th century, probably due to the same kinds of drought-induced crop failure that caused the dispersal of the Ancestral Pueblo and Hohokam cultures of the Southwest at approximately the same time.

AFTER THE HORSE

Epidemics and colonizers swept across the land as soon as the European colonization of the Atlantic coast began. Indigenous communities in the path of "civilization" fled, displacing their neighbours and creating a kind of domino effect in which nearly every Northeast Indian tribe shifted to the west. Eventually groups as far inland as present-day Minnesota and Ontario were displaced westward to the Plains. Among those that eventually resettled on the Plains were the Santee, Yankton, and Teton Sioux and the Saulteaux, Cheyenne, Iowa, Oto, and Missouri.

The convergence of this westward movement with the influx of horses and guns changed Plains life utterly. Horses had entered the region from the Southwest via trade with the Spanish and the expansion of herds of escaped animals. The fur trade was largely responsible for the presence of guns. Plains peoples, whether established residents or newcomers, quickly combined horses and guns to their advantage. Unlike pedestrian hunters, mounted groups could keep pace with the region's large buffalo herds and thereby support themselves on the grasslands. Most hunters initially chose to use bows and arrows in the mounted hunt, as these provided greater accuracy than early guns. However, as firearms became more accurate, they were readily adopted.

APPALOOSA AND CAYUSE

Two horses that are particularly associated with Native Americans are the Appaloosa and the Cayuse. The Appaloosa is a colour breed said to have descended in the Nez Percé Indian territory of North America from wild mustangs, which in turn descended from Spanish horses brought in by explorers. The name derives from the Palouse Indians of Idaho and Washington.

The Appaloosa has several distinctive colour patterns and all of the regular coat colours. Some Appaloosas have a solid colour except for a white patch over the hips, interspersed with small, round spots of the same colour as the body. Others have a basic solid colour with white spots over the entire body or are white with coloured spots. They stand 14.2 to 16 hands (about 57 to 64 inches, or 144 to 163 centimetres) tall and weigh from 1,000 to 1,100 pounds (450 to 500 kilograms).

The small and stocky Cayuse pony had become a distinct breed by the 19th century. It was named for the Cayuse Indians of eastern Washington and Oregon. Although its ancestry has been difficult to establish with certainty, it is thought to have descended from Spanish-Barb horses taken to the New World by the Spanish in the 16th century and to have been cross-bred with Percherons from France that had been imported by French Canadians. The Cayuse is notable for its combination of speed and endurance. Today the breed is relatively rare.

Appaloosa horse. Shutterstock.com

As tribes became more reliant on equestrian hunting, they adjusted their annual round to match that of their primary food source, the buffalo. As a rule, the largest bands or tribes came together en masse only in late spring and summer. During this period the buffalo congregated for calving, allowing hunters to supply enough food to support extensive gatherings of people. During the remainder of the year, the buffalo dispersed into smaller herds, and the nomadic tribes and bands followed suit.

The seasonal round of the village groups may be illustrated by the Arikara, who planted their crops in the spring, spent the summer as nomadic hunters, and returned to their villages in the autumn for the harvest. After a brief period of hunting in the late autumn, they moved to winter hamlets of a few homes each in the wooded bottomlands, which provided shelter from winter storms. They returned to their villages in the spring to begin the cycle anew.

Dogs continued to be used as draft animals, particularly for mundane and short-distance tasks such as hauling water and firewood from a valley to a nearby village or camp. Horses were generally considered too valuable for these activities.

The remainder of this chapter's information on traditional cultures refers to the period after the introduction of the horse.

SHELTER

Tepees were a standard form of shelter for all Plains peoples, although villagers resided for most of the year in earth lodges. As mentioned previously, the tepee is a conical tent, its foundation being either three or four poles. Other poles placed around these formed a roughly circular base. A typical Plains Indian tepee would usually house a two- or three-generation family. The cover was made from dressed buffalo skins carefully fitted and sewn together and often painted with representations of the visions or war exploits of the eldest male resident. Entrance was through an opening in the tent wall, with a flap of the tent covering serving as a door. Early travelers on the Great Plains reported that one scratched or rubbed on the tent wall in lieu of knocking. A hearth in the centre provided heat and light. A smoke hole at the top could be closed in bad weather and in warm weather the sides could be rolled up for additional ventilation. When a large group assembled, a camp circle was usually formed, leaving the space in the centre for ceremonial structures. Among some peoples, such as the Cheyenne and Atsina, each subgroup had a defined place in the circle. Among many tribes, too, the orientation of the lodges and the opening of the circle were toward the rising sun.

The earth lodge, the dwelling used by most village tribes, was much larger than a tepee. Earth lodges averaged 40 to 60 feet (12 to 18 m) in diameter, encompassing approximately 1,250 to 2,825 square feet (116 to 263 sq m), and generally housed three-generation families. Like tepees, they had a roughly circular floor plan. Unlike tepees, they were dome-shaped, roofed and walled with earth, and entered by means of a covered passage. A rattle made of deer hooves often served as a door knocker in these residences. The placement of an earth lodge within a village varied from one tribe to the next and often was determined by the eldest male resident. The homes themselves, however, typically belonged to the women of the household. Earth lodge villages were generally protected by a defensive ditch and palisade.

The construction of Osage and Wichita houses was similar to that of the wickiup of the Northeast culture area. The dwellings of the Osage were oval in ground plan, composed of upright poles arched over on top, interlaced with horizontal withes, and covered with mats or skins. Wichita houses were more conical in shape and thatched with grass. They were otherwise similar in size and occupancy to earth lodges.

CLOTHING, GOODS, AND TRADE

The attire of the men of the northern Plains consisted of a shirt, leggings reaching to the hips, and moccasins. In cold weather, these were worn topped by a buffalo robe painted to depict the owner's deeds in battle. Among the villagers and some southern nomads, men traditionally left the upper part of the body bare and frequently tattooed the chest, shoulders, and arms. Women's clothing typically consisted of a long dress, leggings to the knee, and moccasins. Usually these clothes were decorated with porcupine-quill embroidery, fringe, and in later times, beadwork. Often, the eyeteeth of elk were pierced and used to decorate dresses. As each elk had at most two suitable teeth, a highly decorated dress conspicuously displayed the skill and dedication of the hunters in a woman or girl's family. Billed caps and fur hats were used for protection from the bright sun and the cold. Elaborate headgear and other regalia were reserved for ceremonial occasions.

A round watercraft known as a bullboat, created by stretching a bison skin over a framework of willow withes, was a common vehicle used to transport large quantities of meat or trade goods downstream. Other typical products of the Plains peoples included pipe bowls, usually made of stone but sometimes of clay, and pipe stems, generally of wood. Receptacles of various kinds were made from rawhide, leather, and fascia (sheets of connective tissue surrounding muscle bundles) such as the pericardium

BRIDEWEALTH

The payment made by a groom or his kin to the kin of the bride in order to ratify a marriage is called bridewealth, bride-price, or marriage payment. In cultures that observe this practice, a marriage is not reckoned to have ended until the return of bridewealth has been acknowledged, signifying divorce.

The payment of bridewealth is most often a matter of social and symbolic as well as economic reciprocity, being part of a long series of exchanges between the two intermarrying families. It consolidates friendly relations between them, provides a material pledge that the woman and her children will be well treated, symbolizes her worth to the community, and provides a level of compensation to her natal family for the loss of her labour and company. Bridewealth is often one part of a reciprocal exchange, in which case it is accompanied by the provision of a dowry—a payment presented by the bride's family to that of the groom.

Bridewealth may consist of money or goods, and it may be paid in one sum or in installments over a period of time. The goods transferred may include a diverse array of items such as horses or other livestock, bolts of cloth, drink, food, traditional weapons (such as spears), and vehicles. When the exchange entails the provision of labour to the bride's family, it is known as bride service.

(the membranous sac that holds the heart), which was used as a tough, collapsible bucket. Basketry and pottery were characteristic products of the villagers, although nomadic groups such as the Cheyenne, Comanche, and Arapaho made basketry gambling trays. A few nomadic tribes, such as the Atsina, Blackfoot, and Cree, claimed to have made earthenware in the past but to have given up the practice because the resulting vessels were too fragile for travois transport. Tools were made of fibre, bone, horn, antler, and stone. Many traditional tools, including hide scrapers, cooking vessels, knives, and arrowheads, were made from metal once it became available through the fur trade.

The increased productivity enabled by the horse also brought about differences in wealth. There was a flowering of what one authority has termed luxury developments — "showy clothing, embroidered footgear, medicine-bundle purchases, elaborate rituals [culminating in the Sun Dance], [and especially] gratuitous and time-consuming warfare." Horses became so valuable that horse stealing became a major reason for raiding. In the villages the best horses were even brought inside the earth lodge at night. The man who had many horses could use this wealth for a variety of purposes, such as giving them to those in need, offering them as bridewealth, or trading them for other materials.

Most material goods other than horses were readily available to all members of a given community, and as a result of this there was very little intratribal trade in other goods. Yet there was much exchange of ritual knowledge and other intangibles. Knowledge of war medicine and of curing rites was a valuable asset, and in almost all of the tribes the acquisition of this information was costly. For example, in the 1830s an individual who wished to gain the spiritual benefit believed to accrue from viewing the contents of a Mandan sacred bundle (a group of sacred and ceremonial objects) was expected to pay the bundle's guardian cash, horses, or goods equivalent to about a year's wages for the typical manual labourer. Apprenticeships in craft production were also purchased. Hidatsa customs, for instance, required men who wished to learn to chip flint arrowheads to purchase instruction from the guardians of the bundles associated with arrow-making songs. Similarly, women who wished to learn to make pottery or earth lodges had to purchase apprenticeships from recognized craft and ritual specialists.

Trade between members of different tribes was common and often involved an exchange of products between nomads and villagers, as in the trade of buffalo robes for maize. Intertribal trading relationships were often smoothed by the practice of ritual adoption, as when two men or two women would adopt one another as "brothers" or "sisters." As most social expectations were framed by kinship, adoption defined a clear role for each member of the partnership. The Cheyenne were middlemen in the trade of horses between the tribes of the southern Plains and those of the north-central Plains, while the Assiniboin, Hidatsa, Mandan, Arikara, and later some eastern Sioux groups brokered the guns and other materials such as blankets, beads, cloth, and kettles that flowed from the British and French for pelts and buffalo robes from groups to the west. Conflicts often stemmed from competition among tribes that sought sole control of a specific trade route.

AUTHORITY

The band, rather than the tribe, was the level at which most Plains tribes recognized political authority. Bands were fluid groups that could range in size from a few dozen to a few hundred people who lived, worked, and traveled together. Nomadic tribes generally comprised several large independent bands that coalesced and dispersed over the course of the year. Village groups functioned similarly. A group of related villages might coalesce for a band-level hunt, while smaller groups were the more usual parties for work and socializing.

A band's organization relied upon both individual leaders and military societies. Leaders had to prove themselves beyond their family's social status. Those who were to be entrusted with the community good had to demonstrate individual productivity, wisdom, bravery, and success. Talent and skill played strong roles in leadership as many traditional activities were quite complex—managing a large summer hunt, a communal ritual, a seasonal dispersal, a period of raiding or defense, the building of new earth lodges, or the timing of the planting or the harvesting of a crop—and were often crucial to the group's continued survival. Military societies, in turn, kept the general order and enforced the decisions of leaders.

Each band centred its activities in a loosely defined area within a broader tribal territory. The bands within a tribe did not fight one another, but the degree to which they acted in concert varied. Among the nomadic Comanche, for instance, bands changed membership with ease and the people chose not to have a formal tribal council. Similarly, residency in each of the three Hidatsa villages was quite fluid, but each village nonetheless identified itself as a band and remained politically independent from the others. In contrast, the Skidi band of the Pawnee lived in 19 separate villages that were united in maintaining their political independence from the other three bands within the Pawnee nation. The Cheyenne were the most politically hierarchical Plains group. Their 10 bands sent representatives to a council of 44 peace chiefs, whose decrees were binding on the entire tribe.

DESCENT

There was no usual method of reckoning descent among the Plains peoples. Some cultures reckoned descent bilaterally, or equally in both the male and female lines. Others reckoned descent exclusively in either the male or female line. When descent was unilateral, a child automatically became a member of either the father's or mother's lineage (a group that could trace its ancestry to a known individual) and clan (a group of lineages). This did not mean that there was no recognition of the other parent and his or her relatives. Rather, both parents and their kin usually had specific roles to fill. Frequently a child was treated indulgently by lineal or clan relatives, who taught him ordinary life skills such as hunting (for boys) or agriculture (for girls), while nonlineal relatives were more authoritarian and acted as spiritual mentors.

For example, although the Hidatsa had a matrilineal clan system (using the mother's line to trace descent back to a common female ancestor), a child in this tribe nonetheless had important relationships with the father as well as his clan: always treated with respect and often presented with gifts, paternal kin had important mentoring roles in warfare and ritual performances such as the Sun Dance, and had the privilege of naming children. The Mandan and Crow also had matrilineal clan systems. The patrilineal clan system was characteristic of the Iowa, Kansa, Omaha, Osage, and Ponca, and probably the Blackfoot and Atsina.

MARRIAGE

The rules of marriage varied considerably among Plains Indians. In some tribes certain clans regarded themselves as more closely related to each other than to other clans. Among the Kansa the 16 clans were grouped into 7 larger units (phratries) that regulated marriage and certain other activities. Occasionally phratries were further grouped into two complementary units, or moieties. The Ponca moieties, for instance, were each composed of two phratries, each consisting of two clans. A key feature of the clan system was its ability to transcend band differences within the tribes. One was generally expected to provide hospitality to clan relatives regardless of their band loyalties, which served to strengthen tribal ties in general.

Each group had regulations governing marriage. The Atsina and Blackfoot, for instance, did not tolerate marriage between genetic relatives, no matter how distant the tie. Still others proscribed marriage within varying degrees of relationship. However, unions between those who were already connected through marriage were often preferred. It was common for a man to marry the widow of his deceased brother (a practice known as levirate) or a woman to marry the widower of her deceased sister (sororate). Most marriages were monogamous, although polygyny was also common. Polygynous marriages usually involved sisters sharing a husband, as this built on established bonds and ensured that friendly parties would share in raising the household's children and caring for its elders.

Ideally marriages were arranged between the families of the bride and groom, the latter usually paying bride-wealth. Sometimes, as among the Mandan, this was a purely symbolic exchange as each side provided exactly equivalent gifts. Virginity was highly prized among most of the tribes, particularly the Cheyenne. Among the Blackfoot, women known to be chaste were selected for roles in important ceremonies. A double standard prevailed, however, and men in all of the tribes were expected to pursue sexual conquests. Elopement was not unknown, but attitudes varied. The Teton tolerated the couple on their return, while the Cheyenne considered the girl disgraced forever.

The acceptable behaviour between in-laws was highly regulated by most Plains tribes. Their interactions were typically characterized by avoidance behaviour. This so-called "mother-in-law taboo" in which a man and his wife's mother showed their mutual respect by not speaking to, or in some cases not even looking at, each other was usually paralleled by a "father-in-law taboo," in which a woman and her husband's father would avoid one another for the same reasons. The Atsina and a few other tribes required brothers-in-law to be very circumspect in their speech, avoiding any reference to sex no matter how indirect.

Most Plains tribes also had joking relationships between particular categories of kin. Perhaps the most universally recognized joking relatives were grandparents and grandchildren. Although parents, and especially mothers, were often visibly fond of their children, the latter were expected to treat their parents with respect. In contrast, grandchildren and grandparents often engaged in mild ribbing. When praise for good behaviour proved insufficient, this was the preferred way to remind a child of appropriate comportment. Most kinship systems delineated a wide network of additional joking relatives. Teasing, roughhousing, and practical joking was expected within these cohorts and one was to respond to them in a good-natured manner or risk losing prestige.

SOCIALIZATION AND EDUCATION

Training in socialization began early for Plains children, as part of their play. Grandparents were often depended upon to supervise their grandchildren, and, because of the easy nature of that relationship, the process was usually pleasant. Older children were also charged with watching after their younger counterparts.

The division of labour in Plains tribes was distinct. Women were responsible for producing children, raising and gathering plant foods, constructing and maintaining the home, cooking, and providing clothing and other domestic accoutrements, while men hunted for the household and provided defense for the community. In preparation for her adult role, a young girl would be given a doll to play with and care for. As she grew older her family might make her child-sized hide-scraping tools, which her female relatives would teach her to use. She would learn to sew by making clothes for her doll and to keep house in a child-sized tepee. Likewise, a young boy would be given a child-sized bow and arrows with knobbed tips. As he grew taller and stronger he would receive larger, heavier bows and learn how to stalk small game and to hit moving targets. Groups of boys engaged in shooting matches and play battles, the winners receiving acclaim from their elders. The losers were praised if they had fought bravely. Girls played a game in which a ball was kept in the air without using the hands. Children also engaged in horse races, foot races, swimming, and games of chance.

The young were encouraged to behave in desired ways by praise and reward, with many of the tribes giving special praise for the first successful completion of a task or skill. Thus an Oto father publicly gave away property to honour his son when the boy first walked, when he brought in his first small game, when he killed his first deer, and when he returned from his first war party. When a Crow boy killed his first big game animal, he was given public recognition. A song celebrating the achievement was sung at a ceremony similar to that which would mark his return from a first war party. Progress toward maturity was generally rewarded by removing restrictions and granting special privileges. Blackfoot boys who won shooting matches were allowed to wear feathers in their hair. As soon as he went on his first war party, a Cheyenne boy was relieved from the duty of herding horses and also from the necessity of listening to long lectures on proper behaviour. Girls were similarly recognized for their accomplishments in food production, cooking, quilling, beading, hide processing, and the like. A few tribes, including the Plains Cree, ritually marked the occurrence of the girl's first menses.

In a number of tribes the mother's brother and the father's sister played important roles as mentors and disciplinarians. Among the matrilineal Hidatsa, the maternal uncle was responsible for the direction and supervision of his nephews. He guided them and punished them, but also praised them. Arapaho parents relied on the father's sister to instruct a girl in proper behaviour and to reprimand her if necessary. Physical punishment was seldom employed. Praise and reward for achievement seem to have been generally emphasized more than ridicule and admonishment for failure, although a child's joking relatives were a constant presence and their potential for teasing provided a strong incentive for socially acceptable interaction.

RANK AND WARFARE

The cultural ethos of the traditional Plains peoples interwove expectations of individual competency with those of obligation to the community. Generosity toward the poor, the sharing of goods with relatives, and cooperation with others were honoured qualities, and they enhanced the status of an individual or family.

Although no hereditary social classes existed, individuals were ranked. The son of a wealthy family would have an early advantage over a poor child in that he could rely on his family for the material support necessary to pay for craft and ritual apprenticeships, initiation fees for military societies, bridewealth, and feasts. As time passed, however, such a man would have to prove himself independently. A poor man, in contrast, might spend his youth in straightened circumstances but could win wealth and standing through prowess at war or ritual. In some tribes orphans were the preferred marriage partners, as they

Dancer of the Hidatsa Dog Society, *aquatint by Karl Bodmer, 1834.* Courtesy of the Rare Book Division, the New York Public Library, Astor, Lenox and Tilden Foundations

had proved themselves to be responsible individuals and capable providers at a young age.

War exploits were ranked, but tribes did not evaluate particular deeds in the same way. Intertribal fighting seldom involved major tribal forces. It was carried out mainly by raiding parties of a few warriors to avenge a death, to steal horses, and especially to gain glory, which could be accomplished by counting coup (touching enemies to shame or insult them). Stealing a valuable horse that had been picketed at its owner's lodge was also considered a feat of renown. In many tribes, groups of young boys developed stealth by the socially approved practice of attempting to steal food from their neighbours' lodges. In the event of a group's success, the lodge residents often held a feast in the boys' honour. Such a celebration of the thieves' skill exempted the household from further plunder.

Most tribes had a number of religious and secular associations. Among the latter were military groups such as the Hidatsa Dog Society. These generally functioned as police and sometimes as rivals for battle honours. Among the Crow, for example, there were two outstanding societies, the Lumpwoods and the Foxes, that were of equal

AGE SET

A formally organized group consisting of every male (or female) of comparable age is known as an age set. In those societies chiefly identified with the practice, a person belonged, either from birth or from a determined age, to a named age set that passed through a series of stages, each of which had a distinctive status or social and political role. Each stage is usually known as an age grade.

Among five of the Plains Indians tribes of North America (Blackfoot, Atsina, Arapaho, Mandan, Hidatsa), there were ceremonial societies organized on the age-grading principle. It has been suggested that the prominence of age grading in these tribes (contrasted with its absence among other Plains Indians) may be partly attributable to the absence of any extensive division of labour or economic inequality in these tribes. Whereas such tribes as the Crow had large numbers of horses (in a warring and buffalo-hunting culture that demanded horses) and made their possession the chief basis of individual wealth and social status, the five tribes were relatively poor in horses, and age grades provided the basis of social stratification.

This idea is useful in considering the differences between tribal societies and other forms of society, including modern societies. In the last-named—though age differences are recognized, particularly in youth movements and organizations—there is no formal and elaborate organization of the population in age sets and grades. It may thus be that social classification mainly in terms of gender and age belongs to an early period of social development, when obvious "natural" differences provide a means of differentiation, and that these factors lose their prominence with the more extensive division of labour and the growth of economic inequality.

rank and competed fiercely in feats of war. The Arapaho, Atsina, Blackfoot, Mandan, and Hidatsa ranked their military societies in a series of age sets, groups of individuals of a similar age who functioned as a cohort. Distinctive regalia and membership privileges in each society were purchased collectively by each age set from the next older group, the exchange continuing until the oldest group sold all their materials and retired from the system. The number of societies varied. The Hidatsa at one time had as many as 10 military societies.

Women had their own ritual and secular associations. Where men's groups were generally oriented toward raiding, women's societies generally focused on the fertility of humans, animals, and crops, and on the turning of the seasons. Among the Mandan and Hidatsa, women's societies were also age-graded. It has been reported that such women's societies also existed among the Blackfoot, Arapaho, and Atsina.

RELIGION

To the Plains tribes, there was not a sharp distinction between the sacred and the secular. Nevertheless, they acknowledged that certain objects, such as the contents of sacred bundles, had more supernatural power than others. Much importance was attached to visions, and their cultures generally included aspects of animism, a belief system in which natural phenomena such as animals, plants, the sun, moon, stars, thunder, and lighting are physical manifestations of spirit-beings.

The intervention of these spirit-beings was believed to be responsible for success in life. To entreat their help, individuals usually had to undertake a vision quest, in which they would go to some lonely spot to fast and beg for aid. Men might also mortify the flesh (that is, ritually cut or pierce the skin), though women usually did not. If the suppliant was successful, the spirit-being would provide detailed instructions for winning immunity in battle, curing illness, or obtaining other skills or powers. Those persons who were particularly respectful might gain the protection of a guardian spirit. The quest for supernatural power through a vision or dream was important among all of the tribes and among both girls and boys. Vision quests were often begun when a child was as young as six or seven years of age. Not everyone was successful in the vision quest, and among the Crow and some other tribes those with power were permitted to transfer it to others less fortunate.

All of the tribes had people who communed with the spirit world in order to perform acts of healing and shamanism. In most of the groups ordinary illnesses such as dysentery or headaches would be treated with common herbal remedies, while a shaman would be called in to diagnose and treat more serious illnesses. It was widely believed that illness was caused by intrusion of a foreign object in the body and that the shaman could cure the patient by extracting the item. If the extraction failed, there had presumably been some unwitting infraction of the rules as laid down by the shaman's supernatural sponsor. Shamans were not required to take every case, as their reputation depended upon their ability to cure. Among the Teton they could refuse after examining a patient. Other services they might render included locating enemies and game animals and even finding lost objects. Arapaho, Atsina, and Cheyenne shamans were reported to walk on fire as a proof of their powers.

In some tribes it is difficult to distinguish the role of the shaman, who had direct contact with the supernatural, from that of the priest, who obtained his knowledge from other practitioners. In some cases the two roles were more or less combined. Among the Cheyenne the main road to supernatural power was through acquisition of ritual knowledge from one who was already a priest, although power was also sought through visions. Thus the same individual may have acted in some situations as a shaman and in others as a priest.

Among the tribes having a clear belief in a spirit superior to all other spirits were the Cheyenne, the Atsina, and the Pawnee. The Cheyenne, for instance, held that "the Wise One above" knew better than all other creatures. Further, he had long ago left the Earth and retired to the sky. In smoking ceremonies the first offering of the pipe was always made to him. Some of the other tribes, such as the Crow, believed instead in multiplicity of deities, each of whom possessed more or less equal power.

Ceremonial and ritual were well developed on the Plains. They ranged from very simple rites to complicated proceedings involving weeks of preparation and performances that lasted for several days. A number of common ritual elements were used alone or combined in various ways. Sacred bundles, also called medicine bundles, figured prominently in rituals throughout the area. In some cases the bundle was a personal one, the contents of which had been suggested by a guardian spirit, while in others it was a tribal property with a long, or even mythological, history. Bundles were handled reverently and opened according to definite rules. The opening of the Cheyenne sacred arrow bundle, for instance, was the focus of an elaborate tribal rite extending over four days.

The sacred number for most tribes was four, often said to represent the cardinal directions. A less common number was seven, representing the cardinal direction plus "up" or the sky, "down" or the world below, and "centre" or the location of the ritual. Often dances, songs, or other parts of a ritual were performed in or by groups of four or seven. Many rituals used an altar or other specially prepared space in a ceremonial structure for arranging sacred objects or smoking them with incense. The dimensions of the altar and the symbols that were used varied with

SUN DANCE

The Sun Dance is the most important religious ceremony of the Plains Indians. It formed, for nomadic peoples, an occasion when otherwise independent bands gathered to reaffirm their basic beliefs about the universe and the supernatural through rituals of personal and community sacrifice. The name Sun Dance, though now commonly used, was an inaccurate English name for an intense ceremony of sacrifice and prayer. Traditionally, a Sun Dance was held by each tribe once a year in late spring or early summer, when the buffalo congregated after the long Plains winters. The large herds provided a plentiful food source for the hundreds of individuals in attendance.

The origin of the Sun Dance is unclear. Most tribal traditions attribute its conventions to a time deep in the past. By the end of the 19th century it had spread with local variations to include most of the tribes from the Saulteaux in Saskatchewan, Can., south to

Bull Dance, Mandan O-kee-pa Ceremony, *oil painting by George Catlin, 1832; in the Smithsonian American Art Museum, Washington, D.C.* Courtesy of the Smithsonian American Art Museum (formerly National Museum of American Art), Washington, D.C.

the Kiowa in Texas, U.S., and was common among the settled agriculturists and the nomadic hunting and gathering societies of the region.

The Sun Dance is an example of the globally common religious practice of requesting power or insight from the supernatural. In many instances sun dancing itself was a private experience involving just one or a few individuals who had pledged to undertake the grueling ritual. The development of participation by the whole community, direction by tribal and religious leaders, and elaboration of ceremonies augmenting the votaries' prayers and offerings indicate the ways this ritual reflected a tribe's secular and religious aspirations.

The most elaborate versions of the Sun Dance took place within or near a large encampment or village and required up to a year's preparation by those pledging to dance. Typically the pledges' spiritual mentors and extended families were heavily involved in the preparations, as they were obligated to provide most of the necessary supplies for the ritual. Such supplies generally included payments or gifts to mentors and ritual leaders, often in the form of elaborately decorated clothing, horses, food, and other goods.

As the community gathered, specific individuals—usually members of a particular religious society—erected a dance structure with a central pole that symbolized a connection to the divine, as embodied by the sun. Preliminary dances by a variety of community members often preceded the rigours of the Sun Dance itself, encouraging supplicants and ritually preparing the dance grounds. One such preliminary was the Buffalo Bull Dance, which preceded the Sun Dance during the complex Okipa ritual of the Mandan people.

Those who had pledged to endure the Sun Dance generally did so in fulfillment of a vow or as a way of seeking spiritual power or insight. Supplicants began dancing at an appointed hour and continued intermittently for several days and nights. During this time they neither ate nor drank. In some tribes supplicants also endured ritual self-mortification beyond fasting and exertion. In others such practices were thought to be self-aggrandizing. When practiced, self-mortification was generally accomplished through piercing: mentors or ritual leaders inserted two or more slim skewers or piercing needles through a small fold of the supplicant's skin on the upper chest or upper back. The mentor then used long leather thongs to tie a heavy object such as a buffalo skull to the skewers. A dancer would drag the object along the ground until he succumbed to exhaustion or his skin tore free. Among some tribes the thongs were tied to the centre pole, and the supplicant either hung from or pulled on them until free. Piercing was endured by only the most committed individuals, and, as with the rest of the ritual, it was done to ensure tribal well-being as well as to fulfill the supplicant's individual vow.

In 1883, acting on the advice of Bureau of Indian Affairs personnel, the U.S. secretary of the interior criminalized the Sun Dance and a variety of other indigenous religious practices. Under federal law the secretary was entitled to make such decisions without consulting Congress or the affected parties. The prohibition was renewed in 1904 and reversed in 1934 by a new administration. During the period of prohibition, attenuated forms of the ritual continued among a number of tribes, usually as part of public Fourth of July celebrations. Despite government efforts, the original forms of the Sun Dance were never completely repressed, and in the early 21st century it remained a significant religious ritual among many Plains peoples.

the tribe and the ceremony. Ritual purification in a sweat lodge was required in connection with many ceremonies.

One important ritual found among about 20 tribes is the Sun Dance. The indigenous terms for this ritual varied: the Cheyenne phrase may be translated as "New Life Lodge"; the Atsina term means "Sacrifice Lodge." While the central features were the same among all the tribes, there were many differences in detail. The sacrament was always held in summer, when the whole tribe could gather. Those pledging to undertake the most arduous form of the ritual usually did so in thanks for having been relieved of some grave difficulty.

The ceremony was an annual event among the Teton but occurred at quite irregular intervals among the Crow. The pledger was instructed by a priest or ritual specialist. Weeks or even months were needed for spiritual preparation and to gather the food, gifts, and other materials the pledger and his family were expected to provide. A ceremonial structure was built in the centre of the camp circle (or among the Mandan, in a very large earth lodge dedicated to this and other rituals). Before it was erected, offerings were placed in the fork of the central log. Within the structure was an altar upon which buffalo skulls were laid. The pledger and other participants fasted and danced for several days, praying for power.

Chapter 5

INTERCULTURAL CONTACT

The fur trade had introduced European manufactured goods to the Plains peoples. Guns, metal utensils, axes, knives, blankets, and cloth had filtered into the region long before there was much contact between Europeans and Indians. In some cases the new materials were seen by indigenous peoples as superior to the traditional ones. The durability of brass kettles caused them to be preferred over traditional clay pottery, for instance, as the latter were easily broken and time-consuming to produce. Similarly, glass beads were substituted for porcupine quills and metal tools for stone tools, causing some traditional arts and crafts to decline. Paradoxically, however, some aspects of social life intensified as a result of the fur trade. For example, the new purchasing power ascribed to an old product, buffalo robes, indirectly increased polygyny: women were responsible for dressing hides, so the wives of successful hunters sought to bring new partners into the marriage (often their sisters) to share this arduous work. Religion was affected in a similarly indirect manner, insofar as wealth brought by the fur trade encouraged the more frequent transfer of medicine bundles, driving up the cost of gaining ritual knowledge.

Not until the late 18th century did direct contact with Europeans and Euro-Americans began in earnest. In addition to fur traders and explorers, a number of artists and scientists traveled to the region to acquaint themselves with the indigenous cultures. In the process they created unusually thorough records of those cultures and their responses to colonialism. The 1830s were particularly

Travellers Meeting with Minatarre Indians near Fort Clark, *aquatint by Karl Bodmer, 1842*. Library of Congress, Washington, D.C.

well documented through the journals and paintings created by the pioneering ethnologist Prince Maximilian of Wied-Neuwied and his companion, the Swiss artist Karl Bodmer, as well as the American artist George Catlin.

By the 1840s the opening of the Oregon Trail and other routes across the Plains spurred the burgeoning Homestead Movement in the United States. Discussions of tribal unification began as increasing numbers of Euro-American settlers crossed sovereign territory on the way to California and the Pacific Northwest. Some tribes objected to trespass so strongly that they attacked the travelers.

A major conference between tribal leaders and the U.S. government was convened at Fort Laramie in 1851. The United States desired to delineate which lands were to belong to tribes and which to the United States, to establish an intertribal peace, to allow the development

Sioux Indians at Camp, *painting by George Catlin.* Herbert Orth/ Time & Life Pictures/Getty Images

of transportation systems and supporting fortresses in the region, and to guarantee the safety of settlers en route to the West Coast. The tribes desired to establish legal title to their land and guarantees that such title would be held inviolate. Negotiations were successfully completed and brought a period of relative tranquility to the Plains.

THE PLAINS WARS

A number of circumstances led to a period of particularly fierce conflicts from the early 1850s through the late 1870s between Native Americans and the United States and its Indian allies. Renewed development, particularly an influx of settlers who staked claims under the Homestead Act of 1862, reignited tensions in the region. In the Sioux Uprising of the same year Santee bands that had remained

SAND CREEK MASSACRE

The Sand Creek Massacre, which took place on Nov. 29, 1864, was a surprise attack upon a surrendered, partially disarmed Cheyenne Indian camp in southeastern Colorado Territory by a force of about 1,200 U.S. troops, led by Colonel John M. Chivington. The camp contained several hundred Cheyenne and a few Arapaho. The Cheyenne chief Black Kettle had been negotiating for peace and had camped near Fort Lyon with the consent of its commander, Major Scott Anthony. As the attack began, Black Kettle raised the U.S. flag as well as a white flag, but anywhere from 150 to 500 Indians were massacred, including many women and children. Chivington was at first acclaimed for his "victory," but he was subsequently discredited when it became clear that he had perpetrated a massacre. Indeed, the event is also called the Chivington Massacre. The incident was a chief cause of the Arapaho-Cheyenne war that followed and had far-reaching influence in the Plains Indian wars of the next decade.

in Minnesota sought to drive away settlers whom they felt were encroaching on indigenous lands, although most of the areas in question had been ceded to the United States under previous treaties. By the end of the conflict some 400 settlers, 70 U.S. soldiers, and 30 Santee had been killed and more than 300 Santee men had been sentenced to death by hanging. Pres. Abraham Lincoln later commuted most of these sentences.

From that point onward, relations between the region's nomadic peoples and the United States fell into precipitous decline. The retaliatory efforts by each side of the conflict were plentiful and horrific. Examples include the Sand Creek Massacre (1864), in which Colorado militia attacked a Cheyenne village and killed between 150 and 500 people; the Fetterman Massacre (1866), in which

Teton warriors killed an entire unit of 80 U.S. soldiers; and the Washita River Massacre (1868), in which George Armstong Custer and the 7th Cavalry killed more than 100 Cheyenne. The battles during this period have come to be known collectively as the Plains Wars.

It is worth noting that during this period, the village tribes generally sided with the United States. Many of their young men acted as scouts for the U.S. military. In following this strategy, the village groups were acting in their own best interests and suffered far fewer casualties than the nomads. The nomads had arrived on the Plains only a few generations before and were often seen as interlopers by the villagers. Although specific bands of nomads and villagers had long-standing trade relations, the groups generally viewed one another as enemies. Alliance with the United States enabled Arikara, Hidatsa, Mandan, Pawnee, and other men to gain battle honours against traditional foes without breaking the Fort Laramie treaty's prohibitions against intertribal warfare. Further, many village leaders perceived that the United States would become the regional hegemon and that cooperation with that government was the best strategy for retaining possession of tribal land.

The nomadic tribes created an atmosphere in which many settlers eventually abandoned their claims. A second treaty convention at Fort Laramie, held in 1868, was intended to re-establish the peace and did so for a time. However, the United States abrogated the treaty in 1874, opening the Black Hills to development when gold was discovered there. Conflicts were renewed and ultimately several bands of Sioux and Cheyenne united, annihilating Custer and his 7th Cavalry at the Battle of the Little Bighorn (1876).

Acknowledging that military actions against guerillas who were defending their home territories was a difficult and expensive proposition at best, U.S. policy makers turned to the destruction of the indigenous food supply. Buffalo hunting had already been undertaken on a massive scale by private parties and needed little encouragement to become terribly efficient. As the buffalo disappeared, the Plains Indians began to starve, and by the early 1880s most bands had acceded to confinement on reservations.

SYNCRETISM AND ASSIMILATION

In response to the frustration and despair that characterized the early reservation period, several new religious movements took hold—first the Prophet Dance, then the Ghost Dance movement, and later peyotism. All three were syncretic, combining elements of traditional religions with those of Christianity. The Ghost Dance began as a redemptive movement in the Great Basin culture area but became quite millenarian as it spread to the Plains, where believers danced in the hopes that the settlers would disappear, that the buffalo would return, and that their people would be impervious to attack. Concerns that Ghost Dancing would reignite the Plains Wars led to the massacre at Wounded Knee in 1890, in which more than 200 Miniconjou Sioux were killed by the reconstituted U.S. 7th Cavalry. This was the final major armed engagement of the Plains Wars.

Peyotism, a widely practiced indigenous religious movement, centred on ingesting the mescaline-containing fruit of the peyote cactus for its hallucinogenic effects. Both the government and Christian missionaries made efforts to suppress the practice, but adherents of the peyote religion were incorporated in 1918 as the Native American Church, which continued to be a strong organization in the early 21st century.

The bodies of Sioux Indians slain at the Wounded Knee massacre are buried in a mass grave as soldiers and civilians look on, December 1890. MPI/ Archive Photos/Getty Images

Northern Plains tribes living in what is now Canada were also affected by development and particularly by the political changes that flowed from the British creation of the Dominion of Canada in 1867. The new Canadian government quickly stated its intent to annex the northern Plains, most of which had until then been part of Rupert's Land, a territory of the Hudson's Bay Company. Annexation proceeded without consultation with the area's resident tribes.

Many of the larger, more powerful groups in this region, such as the Plains Cree, Blackfoot, Saulteaux, and Métis, knew that the annexation of land presaged the likely destruction of their way of life. Many had provided refuge to tribes fleeing the conflicts in the United States

PEYOTISM

The most widespread indigenous religious movement among North American Indians and one of the most influential forms of Pan-Indianism is peyotism. The term *peyote* derives from the Nahuatl (Aztec) name *peyotl* for a cactus. The tops of the plants contain mescaline, an alkaloid drug that has hallucinogenic effects. It was used in Mexico in pre-Columbian times to induce supernatural visions and as a medicine.

The various forms of peyotist beliefs combine Indian and Christian elements in differing degrees. Among the Teton, for example, the Cross Fire group uses the Bible and sermons, which are rejected by the Half Moon followers, who, however, teach a similar Christian morality. In general, peyotist doctrine consists of belief in one supreme god (the Great Spirit), who deals with humans through various spirits, which include the traditional waterbird or thunderbird spirits that carry prayers to God. In many tribes peyote itself is personified as Peyote Spirit, considered to be either God's equivalent for the Indians to his Jesus for the whites, or Jesus himself. In some tribes Jesus is regarded as an Indian culture hero returned, as an intercessor with God, or as a guardian spirit who has turned to the Indians after being killed by the whites. Peyote, eaten in the ritual context, enables the individual to commune with God and the spirits (including those of the departed) in contemplation and vision and so to receive from them spiritual power, guidance, reproof, and healing.

and were fully aware of the processes and consequences of colonial expansion. The Métis soon instigated the Red River Rebellion (1869–70). As a result, the Canadian government and the rebels agreed that the latter would have a strong presence in provincial government. Canada's Numbered Treaties were subsequently executed. Similar to the First Treaty of Fort Laramie, these agreements delineated tribal and governmental title to lands and the terms of development in the area, among other things. In 1885 a second rebellion was instigated in response to the repression of local rule, but it was quashed and its leaders hanged or imprisoned.

By the end of the 19th century both the United States and Canada had begun to pursue assimilationist programs designed to replace traditional cultures with Euro-American ways of life. Those sent to implement these programs were often corrupt or incompetent, and even the most professional among them encountered many obstacles: the nomadic groups were loath to become sedentary, cattle were universally derided as a poor substitute for buffalo, and reservation land was often unsuitable for agriculture. Cultivation was traditionally women's work and the basis of their economic empowerment, and women and men alike resisted the change in the division of labour brought by the plow. Confusion resulted when officials insisted on listing families by surnames, which few indigenous peoples used. Additional misunderstandings arose within the matrilineal tribes when Euro-Americans insisted that property should pass from father to son rather than from mother to daughter.

Government-sponsored boarding schools were also given the mission of assimilating indigenous children. Attendance was mandatory and children were forced to leave their homes for months or years at a time. Some staff members used extremely harsh measures to force children to give up their traditional cultures and languages. The extent of abuse that occurred in these institutions, including sexual abuse, is perhaps best represented by the Canadian government's 2006 offer of some $2 billion in reparations to former residential school pupils.

THE STRUGGLE FOR SOVEREIGNTY

Tribal sovereignty was challenged by a number of assimila-tionist U.S. government policies such as those mandating confinement to reservations. Resisting these challenges and regaining self-determination became the defining goal of the Plains tribes in the 20th and 21st centuries. Many tribes in the United States were economically devastated by the Pick-Sloan plan, a post-World War II federal devel-opment program that placed major dams on the Missouri River and numerous smaller dams on its tributaries. This project flooded hundreds of square miles of the tribes' most economically productive land and forced the relo-cation of some 1,000 extended-family households. The dams also created lakes so large that they were difficult to bridge, thus isolating reservation communities whose residents had once been able to visit with relative ease.

Not unlike other rural communities seeding eco-nomic growth, by the late 20th and early 21st centuries, many Plains tribes had instituted formal plans to improve their financial outlook. Many of these plans were designed to resolve common rural development issues, such as underemployment and lack of services, while also insti-tuting programs for cultural revitalization. For instance, when tribal schools were opened to replace the boarding schools, many employed tribal elders to instruct children in indigenous languages. Several tribes implemented buf-falo ranching operations with programs that were hoped to aid in the restoration of the Plains ecosystem. A number of groups own casinos and hotels. Other tribal enterprises include manufacturing, trucking, and construction.

Chapter 6

PLAINS PEOPLES IN FOCUS: SELECTED SIOUAN GROUPS

Among the Plains Indians, the variety of groups speaking Siouan languages is greater than those of other language groups of the Plains. Siouan includes at least five language groups: those of the Gulf Coast region (including Biloxi, Ofo, Tutelo), the upper Missouri River region (including Hidatsa and Crow), the northern Plains (including Dakota, or Sioux proper), the central Plains (Omaha, Osage, Ponca, Kansa, and Quapaw), and the Great Lakes (including Ho-Chunk). The Catawba language of the Carolinas is also usually classified as a Siouan language.

ASSINIBOIN

During their greatest prominence the Assiniboin lived in the area west of Lake Winnipeg along the Assiniboin and Saskatchewan rivers, in what are now the Canadian provinces of Alberta, Saskatchewan, and Manitoba.

The name of the tribe is derived from the Ojibwa (Chippewa) term meaning "one who roasts using stones," and the Assiniboin are thus known as "Stonies" in Canada. Although the Assiniboin spoke a Siouan dialect, Nakota, sometime before the 17th century they had broken with the powerful group of Sioux who spoke the Dakota dialect. Subsequently, the Assiniboin and Dakota engaged in an almost constant cycle of raiding and defense. As a result, the Assiniboin formed an alliance with the Cree, who joined the tribe in activities against the Dakota.

Traditionally, the Assiniboin were great buffalo hunters known for exchanging pemmican (preserved buffalo meat) for firearms and other European goods brought in by traders on the Hudson Bay and the upper Missouri. The continuous encroachment of British and French fur traders and settlers caused the tribe to move gradually westward into the plains of what are now Canada and the U.S. states of Montana and North Dakota, bringing them into confrontation with the Blackfoot over control of the northern Plains.

Assiniboin lived in independent bands, each with its own chief and council. The bands moved their camps frequently in pursuit of buffalo. Before the introduction of horses in the 18th century, bands moved on foot and used dog-drawn travois. Women were responsible for all work related to the lodges (tepees), food preparation, and the production of clothing and other necessities from the buffalo. Men's work involved hunting and battle. Prowess in war consisted of the taking of scalps and horses and of counting coup, or touching the enemy, during battle. War party leaders received their instructions in visions or dreams. In spite of their warrior tradition, or perhaps because of confidence in their defensive capabilities, the Assiniboin were exceptionally friendly with traders. As with many other Plains Indians, their most significant religious ceremony was the Sun Dance. Assiniboin power and prominence were severely reduced by recurrent smallpox epidemics that swept the region in the 1820s and '30s, after which most of the Assiniboin were relocated to reservations.

Early 21st-century population estimates indicated some 7,000 individuals of Assiniboin descent.

CROW

The Crow were historically affiliated with the village-dwelling Hidatsa of the upper Missouri River. They occupied the area around the Yellowstone River and its tributaries, particularly the valleys of the Powder, Wind, and Bighorn rivers in what is now the U.S. state of Montana. They were also called Absaroka or Apsarokee.

Whether lured by horse trading out west, repelled by a dispute over the distribution of meat from a slain buffalo—or both—sometime between the mid-17th and the early 18th century the Crow broke with the Hidatsa and moved westward. Traditional Crow social organization included three bands, which were known as Mountain Crow, River Crow, and Kicked-in-Their-Bellies. The last was most likely an offshoot from the Mountain Crow and remained closely allied to that band.

The buffalo and the horse were the focal point for much of traditional Crow life. From the former they made food, clothing, robes, tepee covers, sinew thread, containers, and shields. The horse provided transportation and, through horse racing and trading, a means of entertainment and exchange. By 1740 the Crow had emerged as middlemen engaged in the trading of horses, bows, shirts, and featherwork to the Plains Village tribes for guns and metal goods. These they traded in turn to the Shoshone in Idaho.

In Crow society women's responsibilities included the processing and preparation of food, housing, and clothing. Women also occasionally engaged in raiding parties, particularly when avenging the death of a close relative. Generally, however, warfare was carried on by men and was largely a matter of raiding for horses. For a man to be ranked as a chief, performance of four insults to the enemy, or coups, was required: leading a war party without losing a Crow life, taking a tethered horse from an enemy camp, striking an enemy with a coupstick (a type of club), and wresting a weapon from an enemy. One man from among a camp's chiefs became the head of the camp.

A basic element in traditional Crow religious life was the vision quest. Through a process involving prayer, solemn vows, fasting in isolation, and, sometimes, piercing the body, a man who attained a vision was "adopted" by a supernatural guardian who instructed him in gathering objects into a medicine bundle. He was permitted to share part of his power with other men who had not received visions and to create replica bundles for them. Women also engaged in vision quests, though we know less about traditional women's rituals because few were recorded in the 19th and early 20th centuries.

The Crow grew tobacco for ritual use. According to their traditions, it had been given to them to overcome their enemies. Unlike other clubs and societies among the Crow, Tobacco Societies involved an entrance fee and an elaborate initiation rite, and they were joined by married couples rather than individuals.

The Crow began to suffer high losses from the Blackfoot and Dakota Sioux as the American colonial frontier expanded and drove those tribes into Crow country. In response to constant threats from these enemies, the Crow sided with the U.S. military in the Plains Wars of the 1860s and '70s. In 1868 they accepted a reservation carved from former tribal lands in southern Montana.

In the early 21st century, population estimates indicated some 15,000 individuals of Crow descent.

HIDATSA

The Hidatsa ("People of the Willow") were also called Minitari or Gros Ventres of the River (or of the Missouri). They once lived in semipermanent villages on the upper Missouri River between the Heart and the Little Missouri rivers in what is now the U.S. state of North Dakota.

Until the late 19th century when the tribe's access to its traditional territory was curtailed by the reservation period, the Hidatsa were a semisedentary people who lived in dome-shaped earth-berm lodges (having earth piled against the exterior walls). They raised maize (corn), beans, squash, and tobacco and made pottery. Hidatsa women raised all the food crops, while tobacco was grown and traded by men. Men also hunted bison and other large game and engaged in warfare.

Traditional Hidatsa social organization was structured around clan lineages, age sets, and other groups, including several military societies for men and a variety of men's and women's religious societies. Descent was traced through the maternal line. As with other Plains Indians, the Sun Dance was the major religious ritual, involving long preparation, sacred vows, prayer, and self-sacrifice.

The Hidatsa language is most closely related to that of the Crow, with whom they were once united. After a dispute over the division of a buffalo carcass sometime between the late 17th and the early 18th centuries, the Crow chose to leave village life and become nomadic equestrians. The two tribes maintained close trading relations and frequently intermarried. In other areas of culture, the Hidatsa and the Mandan most closely resemble each other, a result of more than 400 years of continuous and peaceful association.

In the latter part of the 18th century, there were more than 2,000 Hidatsa who, with the Mandan, occupied a central position in the extensive trading network on the northern Plains. Horses, dressed hides, and buffalo robes, obtained from the nomadic tribes to the west, were exchanged with European traders to the east for guns, knives, and other manufactured goods.

In 1837 a smallpox epidemic so severely reduced Hidatsa and Mandan numbers that the two tribes consolidated into one village in order to mount an effective defense against their traditional enemy, the Sioux. Continual harassment by the Sioux and other enemies caused the Hidatsa and Mandan to move the village to a new location near Fort Berthold. Many Arikara (Caddoan speakers) joined them in 1862, also for purposes of defense. Since 1868 the Hidatsa, Mandan, and Arikara, collectively known as the Three Affiliated Tribes, have lived together on what is now the Fort Berthold Reservation in North Dakota.

In the mid-20th century the Three Affiliated Tribes lost more than one-fourth of their reservation to the waters rising behind the Garrison Dam on the Missouri River. Tribal members, who had been farming in the fertile river bottomlands, were relocated to the arid Plains uplands, deeply depressing the reservation economy. By the late 20th century the Three Affiliated Tribes had established buffalo ranching operations and a casino, returning a level of prosperity to their communities.

Early 21st-century population estimates indicated some 1,500 individuals of Hidatsa descent.

IOWA, MISSOURI, AND OTO

In their historic past the Iowa people, together with the Missouri and the Oto, separated from the Ho-Chunk (Winnebago) and migrated southwestward from north of the Great Lakes to the general area of what is now Iowa before European contact with the New World. The Missouri tribe settled at the confluence of the Grand and Missouri rivers in what is now the U.S. state of Missouri, while the Oto continued to travel up the Missouri and its tributaries to what is now Iowa.

IOWA

Living at the transition point between the territories of the Northeast Indians and the Plains Indians, the traditional Iowa tribal economy combined hunting with agriculture. The people were semisedentary, living in villages, raising maize and other crops, and later trading pelts for European manufactured goods. Iowa houses were domed structures, and the people used tepees when hunting or engaging in other mobile activities. Like the Osage and Kansa, Iowa warriors wore their hair in a scalp lock decorated with deer hair. They recognized three grades of battle exploits: participating in a victorious skirmish, killing an enemy, and decapitating an enemy.

In the mid-18th century the Iowa people were estimated to number 1,100. In 1836 they ceded their lands to the United States and moved to a reservation on what is now the Kansas-Nebraska border. Some were later moved to a reservation in Indian Territory (present-day Oklahoma).

Early 21st-century population estimates indicated more than 2,000 individuals of Iowa descent.

MISSOURI

Jacques Marquette and Louis Jolliet encountered the Missouri tribe on the Missouri River in 1673. When the Missouri were defeated in a war with the Sauk and Fox in 1798, the remnants of the tribe scattered to live with the Osage, Kansa, and Oto. By 1805 some of the Missouri people had reassembled, but another defeat, this time by the Osage, dispersed them among the Oto and Iowa.

Early 21st-century population estimates indicated some 2,500 descendants of the combined Oto and Missouri tribes.

OTO

In 1673, when they were met by the Jacques Marquette expedition, the Oto (Otoe) were living some distance up the Des Moines River in present-day Iowa. The Oto merged with the dwindling Missouri group in 1798. By 1804, when they were encountered by the Lewis and Clark Expedition, they were living near the mouth of the Platte River. A series of treaties, in 1830, 1833, 1836, and 1854, ceded all their lands in Missouri, Iowa, Kansas, and Nebraska—except for a reservation on Big Blue River in southern Nebraska—to the United States government. In 1882, together with the Missouri, the Oto were removed to Indian Territory (present-day Oklahoma), where they were grouped with the Ponca, Pawnee, and Oakland tribes into one agency. The reservation land was later dispersed by means of the Dawes General Allotment Act (1887), whereby parcels of land were distributed to individuals (and could be bought by non-Indians). A lawsuit settled in 1964 compensated the tribe for the lands thus lost. The headquarters of the Otoe Missouria tribe are in Red Rock, Okla., U.S. In the early 21st century, the tribe operated several casinos and convenience stores in the region. Since the turn of the 19th century they also have been called Otoe Missouria.

Early 21st-century population estimates indicated some 2,500 individuals of Oto descent.

KANSA

The Kansa (also spelled Kanza or Konza, also called Kaw) lived along the Kansas and Saline rivers in the central portion of what is now the U.S. state of Kansas. It is thought that the Kansa had migrated to this location from an earlier prehistoric territory on the Atlantic coast. They are related to the Omaha, Osage, Quapaw, and Ponca.

Like many other Plains Indians, the Kansa were traditionally a semisedentary people whose economy combined hunting and farming. Two or three Kansa families might live together in a large dome-shaped earth lodge. Several earth lodges were grouped in villages. Each village was presided over by one or more chiefs chosen for wisdom and bravery. Later, chieftainship became hereditary. Kansa men were notable for carefully plucking all their facial and head hair, except for a scalp lock running along the top and back of the head.

The Kansa religion involved animism and a pantheon of spirit beings, or *wakan*, of differing rank and power. The *wakan* were associated with natural phenomena such as the sun, light, darkness, woods, and grasslands. Adolescent boys undertook a vision quest so that, through a period of isolation and self-denial, they might invoke dreams of the future and connect with supernatural phenomena. Kansa burial customs were well-developed and of considerable complexity. After the women of the tribe had painted the face of the deceased and covered the body with bark and a buffalo robe, it was given directions to the land of the dead. The deceased, accompanied by garments, weapons, pipe, and a supply of food, was placed in a shallow grave on a hill and covered with rock slabs.

In 1846 the Kansa were assigned a reservation at Council Grove (Kansas), their last home before removal to Indian Territory (present-day Oklahoma) in 1873. Before the reservation period their population had been much reduced by recurrent warfare with the Fox, Omaha, Osage, Pawnee, and Cheyenne. Pressure from these groups and from colonial sources—the Spanish, English,

French, and finally U.S. settlers—undermined the Kansa subsistence economy. Their estimated population in the late 18th century was 3,000.

Population estimates in the early 21st century indicated approximately 3,200 individuals of Kansa descent.

MANDAN

The Mandan (who call themselves Numakiki) traditionally lived in semipermanent villages along the Missouri River in what is now the U.S. state of North Dakota. Their oral traditions suggest that they once lived in eastern North America.

Traditional 19th-century Mandan villages, which were stockaded, featured 12 to 100 or more dome-shaped earth lodges. Mandan economy centred on raising maize, beans, pumpkins, sunflowers, and tobacco and on hunting buffalo, fishing, and trading with nomadic Plains tribes. The Mandan also made a variety of utilitarian and decorative items, including pottery, baskets, and painted buffalo robes depicting the heroic deeds of the tribe or of individuals. At this time Mandan culture was one of the richest of the Plains. The tribe hosted many prominent European and American travelers, including American explorers Lewis and Clark, Prussian scientist Prince Maximilian of Wied-Neuwied, and artists Karl Bodmer and George Catlin.

Each Mandan village generally had three chiefs: one for war, one for peace, and one as the day-to-day village leader. Mandan social organization was built upon the ties of kinship and of age sets. It included a wide variety of age- and gender-based societies in which membership was obtained by apprenticeship or purchase. These included social, shamanistic, warrior, harvest, and other groups.

Mandan religion included many ceremonies and rituals that were performed by the various societies. The Okipa was the most complex of these. A four-day ritual requiring lengthy preparation and self-sacrifice by participants, it was an elaboration of the Sun Dance common to many Plains tribes. The Okipa had at least three equally important purposes: to commemorate the tribe's divine salvation from a primordial flood, to call the buffalo and other creatures through communication with their spirit avatars, and to provide a vehicle through which individuals could complete vows made to the Almighty (e.g., in thanks or exchange for curing the sick or preventing death in childbirth or battle). It emphasized community prayer and was punctuated by a series of performances (some ribald) to call powerful spirit-beings to the ritual locale, by self-sacrifice through fasting, exertion, and piercing, and by the giving of gifts from supplicants to their spiritual mentors.

In 1750 there were nine large Mandan villages, but recurrent epidemics of smallpox, whooping cough (pertussis), and other diseases introduced through colonization reduced the tribe to two villages by 1800. In 1837 another smallpox epidemic left only 100 to 150 Mandan survivors. Some of these accompanied the Hidatsa to a new settlement near Fort Berthold in 1845. Others followed later, as did members of the Arikara tribe. The Mandan, Hidatsa, and Arikara eventually became known as the Three Affiliated Tribes.

In the mid-20th century, the Three Affiliated Tribes lost a considerable portion of their reservation to the waters of Lake Sakakawea, which rose behind the newly built Garrison Dam. With the flooding of the river bottoms, on which had been the best agricultural land, many tribal members shifted from agriculture to ranching or off-reservation pursuits.

Population estimates indicated approximately 1,300 Mandan descendants in the early 21st century.

OMAHA

The Omaha, like the Osage, Ponca, Kansa, and Quapaw, spoke a language of the Dhegiha branch of the Siouan language stock. Historians think that the speakers of Dhegiha migrated westward from the Atlantic coast at some point in prehistory and that their early settlements were in the present U.S. states of Virginia and the Carolinas. After a time they moved to the Ozark Plateau and the prairies of what is now western Missouri. There the five tribes separated, with the Omaha and the Ponca moving north to what is now Minnesota, where they lived until the late 17th century. At that time the two tribes were driven farther west by the migrating Dakota Sioux. The Omaha and Ponca separated in present-day South Dakota, with the Omaha moving on to Bow Creek in present-day Nebraska. In 1854, under the pressure of encroaching settlers, the Omaha sold most of their land to the U.S. government. In 1882 the government allotted land in Nebraska that prevented the removal of the tribe to Oklahoma.

As with many other Plains Indian tribes, the traditional Omaha economy combined maize agriculture with hunting and gathering. In spring and autumn the people lived in permanent villages of dome-shaped earth lodges, moving into portable tepees for the hunting seasons. Omaha social organization was elaborate, with a class system of chiefs, priests, physicians, and commoners. Rank was inherited through the male line, although individuals could raise their status by distributing horses and blankets or providing feasts.

Traditional Omaha kinship was organized into 10 clans within two larger groups, representing earth and sky. Earth

SUSETTE LA FLESCHE

(b. 1854, Omaha Reservation, Nebraska [U.S.] — d. May 26, 1903, near Bancroft, Neb., U.S.)

Inshata Theumba, better known as Susette La Flesche, was a Native American writer, lecturer, and activist in the cause of American Indian rights. She was born to an Omaha chief who was the son of a French trader and an Omaha woman and was familiar with both cultures. Though he lived as an Indian, he sent his children to a Presbyterian mission school to provide them with an English-language education. Her sister, Susan, became a physician, and her brother, Francis, an ethnologist. Susette was sent to Elizabeth, New Jersey, to continue her education, and she returned to the Omaha Reservation to teach at a government school.

Using the translation of her Omaha name, "Bright Eyes," La Flesche became involved in her people's struggle for justice. She took up the cause of the Ponca, a tribe related to the Omaha who had been uprooted from their lands by the U.S. government and moved to Oklahoma, where sickness and starvation beset them. When the Ponca chief, Standing Bear, and several of his followers returned to Nebraska in 1879 after a long and arduous journey, they were arrested. In April a habeas corpus hearing brought about at the instigation of Thomas H. Tibbles of the *Omaha Herald* resulted in the release of the Ponca and the establishment of a legal precedent in recognizing Native Americans as persons before the law. She then undertook a lecture tour of the eastern United States with Standing Bear, also acting as his interpreter. The tour aroused sympathy in influential circles, led by such individuals as clergyman Edward Everett Hale, anthropologist Alice Fletcher, abolitionist Wendell Phillips, and educator and reformer Mary L. Bonney, and eventuated in the passage of the Dawes General Allotment Act in 1887. In 1881 La Flesche married Tibbles. She continued to work against the arbitrary removal of Indians from their traditional lands, lecturing throughout the United States and in Scotland.

La Flesche and her husband settled on the Omaha Reservation, where she wrote and illustrated Indian stories and helped her husband with his editorial work. She edited and wrote the introduction for *Ploughed Under: The Story of an Indian Chief* (1881), an anonymous work.

clans had charge of ceremonies concerning war and food supply, while the ceremonies overseen by the sky clans were designed to secure supernatural aid. When the entire tribe camped together during the summer bison hunt or on migrations, tepees were arranged in a large circle symbolizing the tribal organization. The Omaha, like many other Plains peoples, awarded special insignia for such daring war exploits as touching an enemy in battle, touching a dead enemy surrounded by his tribesmen, and removing a trained horse from the enemy's camp. Killing the enemy was considered a lesser exploit.

Early 21st-century population estimates indicated more than 5,000 individuals of Omaha descent.

OSAGE

The name Osage is a French alliteration of the name Wazhazhe, one of the two ancient kin groups (the other was the Tsishu) from which the tribe descended. Like other members of the Dhegiha—the Omaha, Ponca, Kansa, and Quapaw—the Osage migrated westward from the Atlantic coast, settling first in the Piedmont Plateau between the James and Savannah rivers in the present states of Virginia and the Carolinas. After a time they moved to the Ozark Plateau and the prairies of what is now western Missouri. At this point the five tribes separated, with the Osage remaining in villages on the Osage River, where Jacques Marquette recorded their location

Osage man wearing traditional regalia, photograph by William J. Boag, c. *1909.* Library of Congress, Washington, D.C.; photograph, Wm. J. Boag (neg. no. LC-USZ62-119215)

in 1673. They remained there until the early 19th century, when they ceded their Missouri lands to the United States government and moved west to the Neosho River valley in Kansas. After settling on the Kansas reservation, the Osage were notable for their persistent rejection of the dominant American culture. They continued to dress in traditional clothing and to build traditional homes. They

MARIA AND MARJORIE TALLCHIEF

(b. Jan. 24, 1925, Fairfax, Okla., U.S.) ; (b. Oct. 19, 1927, Fairfax, Okla., U.S.)

Dancer Maria Tallchief adjusts a ceremonial headdress in preparation for a celebration of her hometown, c. 1953. A.Y. Owen/ Time & Life Pictures/Getty Images

The Tallchief sisters were both ballet dancers of exceptional technique. Born in a town on an Osage Indian reservation in Oklahoma, Maria and Marjorie were of Osage and Scotch-Irish descent. Both sisters began dancing as children and later studied with Bronislava Nijinska and David Lichine, among others.

In 1942 Maria joined the Ballet Russe de Monte Carlo. Over the next five years she attracted much attention with her performances in *Chopin Concerto, Scheherezade, Etude,* and *Le Baiser de la fée.* She created roles in George Balanchine's *Danses concertantes* (1944) and *Night Shadow* (1946), and in 1946 she and Balanchine married (divorced 1952). They left the Ballet Russe early in 1947 and, after a few months as guest artists with the Paris Opéra Ballet, joined the new Ballet Society, which the next year became the New York City Ballet (NYCB).

In her 18 years with that company Maria was the foremost exponent of Balanchine's choreography, and she was the company's prima ballerina in 1954–55. In 1960 she joined the American Ballet Theatre (ABT), but she returned to the NYCB three years later. Her performances in *The Firebird, Orpheus, The Nutcracker,*

Sylvia pas de deux, Scotch Symphony, Pas de dix, and *The Ground Symphony* are among her most highly acclaimed. She retired from the NYCB in 1965. She then served as artistic director of the Lyric Opera Ballet in Chicago and occasionally taught. From 1980 to 1987 (when the company folded) Maria was the artistic director of the Chicago City Ballet, which she founded. In 1996 she was inducted into the National Women's Hall of Fame, and that year she also received a Kennedy Center Honor. *Maria Tallchief: America's Prima Ballerina* (1997) is her autobiography.

Marjorie Tallchief began her professional career in 1944 with the ABT. Two years later she joined the Ballet Russe de Monte Carlo and reunited briefly with her sister there. Marjorie left that company the following year, as did Maria, and between 1947 and 1957 Marjorie danced with the Ballet de Marquis de Cuevas. She joined the Paris Opéra Ballet in 1957, with whom she was associated, most notably as the company's *première danseuse étoile*, until 1962. In 1964–66 she danced with the Harkness Ballet in New York City.

Majorie's most famous roles included those in *Annabel Lee*, *Romeo and Juliet*, *Camille*, *Pastorale*, and *Ariadne*.

also discouraged the use of alcohol, which had been introduced by traders.

Traditional Osage culture was typical of many Plains Indians and involved a combination of village-based agriculture and nomadic bison hunting. Other important game animals were deer, bear, and beaver. Osage villages consisted of longhouses covered with mats or skins and arranged irregularly about an open space used for dances and council meetings. Tepees were used during the hunting season. Osage life centred on religious ceremonials in which clans were divided into symbolic sky and earth groups, with the latter further subdivided to represent dry land and water. The Osage were remarkable for their poetic rituals. Among them was the custom of reciting the history of the creation of the universe to each new-born infant.

Following the American Civil War (1861–65), pressure on the U.S. government to open all Native American lands to emigrant settlement resulted in the sale of the Kansas reservation. The proceeds were used to purchase land for the Osage in Indian Territory (present-day Oklahoma). The discovery of oil on the Osage reservation in the late 19th century and an agreement with the U.S. government by which all mineral rights on the reservation were to be retained by the tribe, with royalties divided on a per capita basis, made the Osage quite prosperous.

Early 21st-century population estimates indicated some 16,000 individuals of Osage descent.

PONCA

An early estimate of Ponca population places their number at 800 individuals. Perhaps because of their small population, they have moved frequently over the past several centuries. Their original locale is thought to have been in what is now the U.S. state of Virginia, from which they moved in turn to the present states of North and South Carolina, western Missouri, and Minnesota. They left Minnesota in the late 17th century owing to incursions by the Dakota Sioux.

Eventually they established homes in what are now southwestern Minnesota and the Black Hills of South Dakota. Like many other Plains Indians, they resided in semipermanent agricultural villages and lived in earth lodges. During the spring and autumn hunting seasons they engaged in communal bison hunts and camped in tepees.

By 1804, when they were encountered by Lewis and Clark, a smallpox epidemic had reduced the tribe to about 200 individuals. In 1865 the Ponca were guaranteed a reservation on their homelands, but after bureaucratic blundering the land was awarded to the Dakota, and the Ponca were forcibly removed to Indian Territory (present-day Oklahoma). The tribe found living conditions there unbearable, and, led by Chief Standing Bear, they traveled north on foot for 600 miles (965 km) to eastern Nebraska, where they received asylum from the Omaha. Many Ponca were arrested for leaving their assigned territory but were freed after Susette La Flesche convinced a group of wealthy and influential individuals to defend the Ponca cause in court. The tribe later moved back to Oklahoma.

In the early 21st century Ponca descendants numbered approximately 5,000 individuals.

QUAPAW

With the other members of the Dhegiha branch of Siouan language speakers, the Quapaw migrated westward from the Atlantic coast. They settled for a time in what is now western Missouri and later relocated at or near the mouth of the Arkansas River. (They are also called Akansa or Arkansas.) They were a sedentary, agricultural people who lived in fortified villages of communal bark-covered lodges built on mounds. They were also skillful artisans noted for their red-on-white pottery.

In 1673 explorers Jacques Marquette and Louis Jolliet reported that the Quapaw did not hunt buffalo for fear of the peoples to the north and west, wore few clothes, and pierced their ears and noses. In 1818 the Quapaw ceded their lands, except for a tract on the southern side of the Arkansas River, to the United States. A few years later this land was opened to emigrant settlers, and most of the tribe relocated to the Red River in present Louisiana. When floods drove them out of this region, they began an unsuccessful campaign for the return of their original lands. In the mid-19th century they settled on their own reservation in Indian Territory (now Oklahoma), but during the American Civil War their land was so overrun by forces from both sides that tribal members fled en masse to Kansas to the reservation of the Ottawa. Most of the Quapaw later returned to their Oklahoma land, which was allotted among them by themselves.

Early 21st-century population estimates indicated more than 2,000 individuals of Quapaw descent.

SIOUX

The name Sioux is an abbreviation of Nadouessioux ("Adders"; i.e., enemies), a name originally applied to them by the Ojibwa. The Santee, or Eastern Sioux, were Dakota speakers and comprised the Mdewkanton, Wahpeton, Wahpekute, and Sisseton. The Yankton, who spoke Nakota, included the Yankton and Yanktonai. The Teton, or Western Sioux, spoke Lakota and had seven divisions—the Sihasapa, or Blackfoot; Brulé (Upper and Lower); Hunkpapa; Miniconjou; Oglala; Sans Arcs; and Oohenonpa, or Two-Kettle.

THE SIOUX WAY OF LIFE

Before the middle of the 17th century, the Santee Sioux lived in the area around Lake Superior, where they gathered wild rice and other foods, hunted deer and buffalo, and speared fish from canoes. Prolonged and continual warfare with the Ojibwa to their east drove the Santee into what is now southern and western Minnesota, at that time the territory of the agricultural Teton and Yankton. In turn, the Santee forced these two groups from Minnesota into what are now North and South Dakota. Horses were becoming common on the Plains during this period, and

Sioux war dance, chromolithograph c. *1890.* Universal Images Group/ Hulton Archive/Getty Images

the Teton and Yankton abandoned agriculture in favour of an economy centred on the nomadic hunting of bison.

Traditionally the Teton and Yankton shared many cultural characteristics with other nomadic Plains Indian societies. They lived in tepees, wore clothing made from leather, suede, or fur, and traded buffalo products for maize produced by the farming tribes of the Plains. The Sioux also raided those tribes frequently, particularly the Mandan, Arikara, Hidatsa, and Pawnee, actions that eventually drove the agriculturists to ally themselves with the U.S. military against the Sioux tribes.

THE SIOUX BEFORE EUROPEAN CONQUEST

Sioux men acquired status by performing brave deeds in warfare. Horses and scalps obtained in a raid were evidence of valour. Sioux women were skilled at porcupine-quill and bead embroidery, favouring geometric designs. They also produced prodigious numbers of processed bison hides during the 19th century, when the trade value of these "buffalo robes" increased dramatically. Community policing was performed by men's military societies, the most significant duty of which was to oversee the buffalo hunt. Women's societies generally focused on fertility, healing, and the overall well-being of the group. Other societies focused on ritual dance and shamanism.

Religion was an integral part of all aspects of Sioux life, as it was for all Native American peoples. The Sioux recognized four powers as presiding over the universe, and each power in turn was divided into hierarchies of four. The buffalo had a prominent place in all Sioux rituals. Among the Teton and Santee the bear was also a symbolically important animal. Bear power obtained in a vision was regarded as curative, and some groups enacted a ceremonial bear hunt to protect warriors before their departure on a raid. Warfare and supernaturalism were closely connected, to the extent that designs suggested in mystical visions were painted on war shields to protect the bearers from their enemies. The annual Sun Dance was the most important religious event.

How the West Was Lost

Having suffered from the encroachment of the Ojibwa, the Sioux were extremely resistant to incursions upon their new territory. Teton and Yankton territory included the vast area between the Missouri River and the Teton Mountains and between the Platte River on the south and the Yellowstone River on the north (e.g., all or parts of the present-day states of Montana, North Dakota, South Dakota, Nebraska, Colorado, and Wyoming).

This territory was increasingly broached as the colonial frontier moved westward past the Mississippi River in the mid-19th century. The California Gold Rush of 1849 opened a floodgate of travelers, and many Sioux became incensed by the U.S. government's attempt to establish the Bozeman Trail and other routes through the tribes' sovereign lands.

The United States sought to forestall strife by negotiating the First Treaty of Fort Laramie (1851) with the Sioux and other Plains peoples. The treaty assigned territories to each tribe throughout the northern Great Plains and set terms for the building of forts and roads within the region. In accordance with the treaty the Santee Sioux gave up most of their land in Minnesota in exchange for annuities and other considerations. They were restricted to a reservation and encouraged to take up agriculture, but government mismanagement of the annuities, depleted game reserves, and a general resistance to an agricultural lifestyle combined to precipitate starvation on the reservation by 1862. That year, with many settler men away fighting the Civil War, Santee warriors under the leadership of Chief Little Crow mounted a bloody attempt to clear their traditional territory of outsiders. U.S. troops soon pacified the region, but only after more than 400 settlers, 70 U.S. soldiers, and 30 Santee had been killed. More than 300 Santee were condemned to death for their roles in what had become known as the Sioux Uprising. Although President Lincoln commuted the sentences of most of these men, 38 Santee were ultimately hanged in the largest mass execution in U.S. history. After their defeat the Santee were relocated to reservations in Dakota Territory and Nebraska.

Although the Native peoples of the Plains had putatively accepted some development in the West by agreeing to the terms of the First Treaty of Fort Laramie, many were

CRAZY HORSE

(b. c. 1842, near present-day Rapid City, South Dakota, U.S.—d. Sept. 5, 1877, Fort Robinson, Nebraska)

Ta-sunko-witko, better known in U.S. history books as Crazy Horse, was a Sioux Indian chief of the Oglala tribe, an able tactician and determined warrior in the Sioux resistance to the white man's invasion of the northern Great Plains.

As early as 1865 Crazy Horse was a leader in his people's defiance of U.S. plans to construct a road to the goldfields in Montana. He participated in the massacre of Captain William J. Fetterman and his troop of 80 men (Dec. 21, 1866) as well as in the Wagon Box fight (Aug. 2, 1867), both near Fort Phil Kearny, in Wyoming Territory. Refusing to honour the reservation provisions of the Second Treaty of Fort Laramie (1868), Crazy Horse led his followers to unceded buffalo country, where they continued to hunt, fish, and wage war against enemy tribes as well as whites.

When gold was discovered in the Black Hills, Dakota Territory, in 1874, prospectors disregarded Sioux treaty rights and swarmed onto the Indian reservation there. General George Crook thereupon set out to force Crazy Horse from his winter encampments on the Tongue and Powder rivers in Montana Territory, but the chief simply retreated deeper into the hills. Joining Cheyenne forces, he took part in a surprise attack on Crook in the Rosebud valley (June 17, 1876), in southern Montana, forcing Crook's withdrawal.

Crazy Horse then moved north to unite with the main Sioux encampment of Chief Sitting Bull on the banks of the Little Bighorn River, where he helped annihilate a battalion of U.S. soldiers under Lieutenant Colonel George A. Custer (June 25, 1876). Crazy Horse and his followers then returned to the hill country to resume their old ways. He was pursued by Colonel Nelson A. Miles in a stepped-up army campaign to force all Indians to come to the government agencies. His tribe weakened by cold and hunger, Crazy Horse finally surrendered to General Crook at the Red Cloud Agency in Nebraska on May 6, 1877. Confined to Fort Robinson, he was killed in a scuffle with soldiers who were trying to imprison him in a guardhouse.

soon dissatisfied with the extent of encroachment on their land. In 1865–67 the Oglala chief Red Cloud led thousands of Sioux warriors in a campaign to halt construction of the Bozeman Trail. In December 1866, warriors under Chief High Backbone drew a U.S. military patrol from Fort Phil Kearny into an ambush. The patrol's commanding officer, Capt. William J. Fetterman, ignored warnings that the Sioux often used apparently injured riders as decoys to draw their enemies into poorly defensible locations. Fetterman led his men in chase of such a decoy, and the entire group of 80 U.S. soldiers was killed. The decoy was Crazy Horse, already displaying the characteristics that later made him a major military leader among his people. The worst U.S. defeat on the Plains to that point, the so-called Fetterman Massacre reignited the anti-Indian sentiment that had flared in the eastern states after the Sioux Uprising of 1862.

The terms of the Second Treaty of Fort Laramie (1868) implicitly acknowledged that the West was proving a very expensive and difficult place to develop. The United States agreed to abandon the Bozeman Trail and guaranteed the Sioux peoples exclusive possession of the present state of South Dakota west of the Missouri River. When gold was discovered in the Black Hills of South Dakota in the mid-1870s, however, thousands of miners disregarded the treaty and swarmed onto the Sioux reservation, thus precipitating another round of hostilities.

The best-known event of the conquest of the American West was the Battle of the Little Bighorn. This painting by Sioux artist Amos Bad Heart Buffalo, c. 1900, depicts the retreat of the 7th Cavalry battalions under Maj. Marcus Reno. The outcome of the battle so stunned and enraged white Americans that government troops flooded the area, forcing the Indians to surrender. Universal Images Group/Hulton Archive/Getty Images

THE BATTLE OF THE LITTLE BIGHORN AND ITS AFTERMATH

The much-discussed Battle of the Little Bighorn, while a resounding Native American win over federal troops, was a case of winning the battle but losing the war. In June 1876, a large contingent of Sioux and Cheyenne warriors took advantage of the hubris of U.S. officers, overwhelming Lieut. Col. George A. Custer and 200 men of his 7th Cavalry. This definitive indigenous victory essentially sealed the fate of the tribes by instigating such shock and horror among American citizens that they demanded unequivocal revenge. The so-called Plains Wars essentially

Eighty years after the 1876 Battle of the Little Bighorn (also called Custer's Last Stand), a Sioux veteran of the famed confrontation gives his account of the momentous day's events. Bates Littlehales/National Geographic Image Collection/Getty Images

ended later in 1876, when American troops trapped 3,000 Sioux at the Tongue River valley. The tribes formally surrendered in October, after which the majority of members returned to their reservations.

Although most of the Sioux bands had surrendered, the chiefs Sitting Bull, Crazy Horse, and Gall refused to take their people to the reservations. Crazy Horse surrendered in 1877 only to be killed later that year while resisting arrest for leaving the reservation without authorization. He was reportedly transporting his ill wife to her parents' home. Sitting Bull and Gall escaped to Canada for several years, returning to the United States in 1881 and surrendering without incident.

The Sioux were among those who in 1890–91 were highly influenced by the Ghost Dance movement, which promised the coming of a messiah, the disappearance of all people of European descent from North America, the return of large buffalo herds and the lifestyle they supported, and reunion with the dead. The new religion held great appeal, as most of the Sioux bands had suffered harsh privations while confined to reservations: game had all but disappeared; the supplies and annuities promised in treaties were frequently stolen by corrupt officials; and many people lived almost continuously on the verge of starvation. Believing that the Ghost Dance movement threatened an already uneasy peace, U.S. government agents set out to arrest its leaders. In 1890 Sitting Bull was ordered to stay away from Ghost Dance gatherings. He stated that he intended to defy the order and was killed as Lakota policemen attempted to take him into custody. When the revitalized U.S. 7th Cavalry—Custer's former regiment—massacred more than 200 Sioux men, women, and children at Wounded Knee Creek later that year, the Sioux ceased military resistance.

The warrior ethic continued among the Siouan tribes throughout the 20th century, with many people—women as well as men—serving in the U.S. military. However, Sioux individuals did not take up arms against the U.S. government again until 1973, when a small group of American Indian Movement members occupied the community of Wounded Knee, exchanging gunfire with federal marshals who demanded their surrender.

Early 21st-century population estimates indicated some 160,000 individuals of Sioux descent.

Chapter 7

PLAINS PEOPLES IN FOCUS: SELECTED ALGONQUIAN AND OTHER LANGUAGE GROUPS

A part from the Siouan language family, the Plains Indians spoke Algonquian, Caddoan, Athabaskan, Kiowa-Tanoan, and Uto-Aztecan languages. As mentioned previously, Michif and Plains Indian sign language were also significant.

ALGONQUIAN SPEAKERS

The languages of the Algonquian (Algonkian) language family are or were spoken in Canada, New England, the Atlantic coastal region southward to North Carolina, and the Great Lakes region and surrounding areas westward to the Rocky Mountains. Among them are Cree, Ojibwa, Blackfoot, Cheyenne, Mi'kmaq (Micmac), Arapaho, and Fox-Sauk-Kickapoo.

ARAPAHO

During the 19th century, the Arapaho lived along the Platte and Arkansas rivers of what are now the U.S. states of Wyoming, Colorado, Nebraska, and Kansas. Their oral traditions suggest that they once had permanent villages in the Eastern Woodlands, where they engaged in agriculture. Because of pressure from tribes to the east, the Arapaho gradually moved westward, abandoning farming and settled life during the process. They split into northern (Platte River) and southern (Arkansas River) groups after 1830.

111

As was the case with many tribes that made the westward trek, the Arapaho became nomadic equestrians, living in tepees and depending on buffalo hunting for subsistence. They also gathered wild plant foods and traded buffalo products for maize (corn), beans, squash, and European manufactured goods. Their main trading partners were the farming Mandan and Arikara tribes in what are now North and South Dakota and the Spanish in the Southwest.

For the Arapaho, who were traditionally a deeply religious people, symbolic meaning was to be found in everything from everyday actions to objects (such as beadwork designs). Their chief object of veneration was a flat pipe that was kept in a sacred bundle with a hoop or wheel. The Arapaho practiced the Sun Dance, and their social organization included age-graded military and religious societies.

From early times the Arapaho were continually at war with the Shoshone, the Ute, and the Pawnee. The southern Arapaho were for a long period closely associated with the southern Cheyenne. Some Arapaho fought with the Cheyenne against Lt. Col. George Armstrong Custer at the Little Bighorn in 1876. In the Treaty of Medicine Lodge in 1867, the southern Arapaho were assigned a reservation in Oklahoma together with the Cheyenne, while the northern Arapaho were assigned a reservation in Wyoming with the Shoshone.

Early 21st-century population estimates indicated some 15,000 individuals of Arapaho descent.

ATSINA

The Atsina are related to the Arapaho, from whom they may have separated as early as 1700. Their variant name

Gros Ventres (French: "Big Bellies") was a misinterpretation by French trappers of Plains Indian sign language. The Blackfoot called the Atsina the "Belly People," and the sign for that name was similar to one referring to the chest tattooing practiced by a neighbouring subgroup of unrelated Hidatsa, also known as the Gros Ventres de la Riviere ("of the River"). The Atsina were thereafter distinguished from the Hidatsa with the addition of "des Plaines" ("of the Prairie") to their misnomer. Their self-name, A'aninin, means "White Clay People."

The Atsina were living in what is now northern Montana and adjacent regions of Canada in late-prehistoric times and were culturally similar to other Plains tribes. Their language was unusual in having different pronunciations for men and women. The Atsina were mentioned in the journals of the Lewis and Clark Expedition (1804–06). In the late 1800s they were relocated to Fort Belknap Reservation in northern Montana, which they shared with the Siouan-speaking Assiniboin. Atsina descendants numbered more than 6,000 in the early 21st century.

BLACKFOOT

Three closely related bands, the Piegan (official spelling in Canada is Peigan), or Pikuni; the Blood, or Kainah; and the Siksika, or Blackfoot proper (often referred to as the Northern Blackfoot) constitute the Blackfoot. The three groups traditionally lived in what is now Alberta, Can., and the U.S. state of Montana, and there they remain, with one reservation in Montana and three reserves (as they are called in Canada), one for each band, within Alberta. The Blackfoot in the United States are officially known as the Blackfeet Nation, though the Blackfoot word *siksika*, from which the English name was translated, is not plural.

Blackfoot on horseback, engraving after drawing by Swiss artist Karl Bodmer, c. 1832. Bodmer created this and other pictures during an expedition to observe Indians of the American West led by German ethnographer and explorer Maximilian of Wied-Neuwied. Apic/Hulton Archive/ Getty Images

The Blackfoot are among the few tribes that continue to live on their ancestral territory.

Having most likely migrated on foot using dog-drawn wooden travois to transport their possessions, the Blackfoot were among the first Algonquian-speakers to move westward from timberland to open grassland. In the early 18th century they were pedestrian buffalo hunters living in the Saskatchewan valley about 400 miles (645 km) east of the Rocky Mountains. They acquired horses and firearms before 1750. Driving weaker tribes before them, the Blackfoot pushed westward to the Rockies and southward into what is now Montana. At the height of their power, in the first half of the 19th century, they held a vast territory extending from northern Saskatchewan to the southernmost headwaters of the Missouri River.

Known as one of the strongest and most aggressive military powers on the northwestern Plains, for a quarter of a century after 1806, the Blackfoot prevented British, French, and American fur traders, whom they regarded as poachers, from trapping in the rich beaver country of the upper tributaries of the Missouri. At the same time, they warred upon neighbouring tribes, capturing horses and taking captives.

Each Blackfoot tribe was divided into several hunting bands led by one or more chiefs. These bands wintered separately in sheltered river valleys. In summer they gathered in a great encampment to observe the Sun Dance, the principal tribal religious ceremony. Many individuals owned elaborate medicine bundles—collections of sacred objects that, when properly venerated, were said to bring success in war and hunting and protection against sickness and misfortune.

A treaty of 1855 established the Blackfoot Indian Reservation in northwestern Montana. For three decades after this treaty was made, the Blackfoot declined to forsake hunting in favour of farming. When the buffalo were almost exterminated in the early 1880s, nearly one-quarter of the Piegan died of starvation. Thereafter the Blackfoot took up farming and ranching.

The Blackfoot Confederacy in Canada signed a treaty with the Canadian government in 1877, which granted three reserves—one each for the Peigan, Blood, and Blackfoot—in southern Alberta, though a few decades later, the government sold half of the Blackfoot reserve.

Early 21st-century population estimates indicated some 90,000 individuals of Blackfoot descent in Canada and the United States.

CROWFOOT

(b. c. 1836, near Belly River, Alta., Can. — d. April 25, 1890, Blackfoot Crossing, near Calgary, District of Alberta, Can.)

Sahpo Muxika, better known to English speakers as Crowfoot, was the head chief of the Blackfoot tribe of Indians and a strong advocate of peace and subservience to whites.

Crowfoot was only 13 years old when he took part in his first raid. He became a noted warrior and eventually was appointed head chief of the Blackfoot. He tried to discourage tribal warfare, and he refused to join other Indians in attacks against the North West Mounted Police. The Canadian Pacific Railway pensioned him for keeping peace when survey parties attempted to cross western Canada in 1883. During the 1885 Northwest Rebellion—an uprising of Métis (persons of mixed European and Indian ancestry) and Plains Indians against the Canadian government—Crowfoot refused to submit to heavy pressure from his tribe and his adopted son Poundmaker to join with the rebels.

CHEYENNE

The Cheyenne were North American Plains Indians who spoke an Algonquian language and inhabited the regions around the Platte and Arkansas rivers during the 19th century. Before 1700 the Cheyenne lived in what is now central Minnesota, where they farmed, hunted, gathered wild rice, and made pottery. They later occupied a village of earth lodges on the Cheyenne River in North Dakota. It was probably during this period that they acquired horses and became more dependent on the buffalo for food.

Following the destruction of their town by the Ojibwa (Chippewa), the Cheyenne settled along the Missouri River near the Mandan and Arikara tribes. Toward the

close of the 18th century, smallpox and the aggression
of the Dakota Sioux decimated the village tribes at the
same time that the horse and gun were becoming generally available in the northeastern Plains. The Cheyenne
moved farther west to the area of the Black Hills, where
they developed a unique version of nomadic Plains culture
and gave up agriculture and pottery. During the early 19th
century, they migrated to the headwaters of the Platte
River in what is now Colorado. In 1832 a large segment of
the tribe established itself along the Arkansas River, thus
dividing the tribe into northern and southern branches.
This division was recognized in the First Treaty of Fort
Laramie with the United States in 1851.

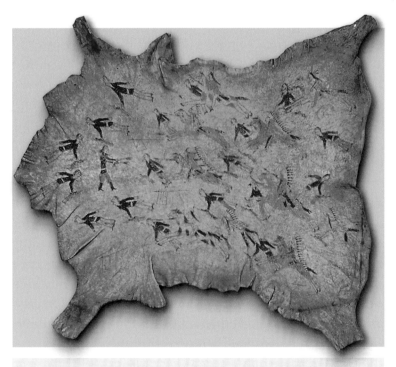

*Painted buffalo hide depicting the Battle of the Little Bighorn, by a Cheyenne
artist, c. 1878; in the George Gustav Heye Center of the National Museum
of the American Indian, New York City.* Courtesy of the Museum of the
American Indian, Heye Foundation, New York

Traditional Cheyenne religion focused upon two principal deities, the Wise One Above and a god who lived beneath the ground. In addition, four spirits lived at the points of the compass. The Cheyenne performed the Sun Dance in a very elaborate form. They placed heavy emphasis on visions in which a guardian spirit adopted the individual and bestowed special powers upon him or her so long as certain prescribed laws or practices were observed. Their most-venerated objects, contained in a sacred bundle, were a hat made from the skin and hair of a buffalo cow and four arrows—two painted for hunting and two for battle. These objects were carried in war to ensure success over the enemy.

Traditional Cheyenne society was organized into 10 major bands governed by a council of 44 chiefs and 7 military societies; the Dog Soldiers were the most powerful and aggressive of the military groups. There were also social, dance, medicine, and shamanistic societies. A given society was generally open to either male or female members but not to both.

The Cheyenne fought constantly with the Kiowa until 1840, when a lasting peace was established between them. From 1857 to 1879 the Cheyenne were embroiled in raids and wars with U.S. military troops. These conflicts often caused suffering for civilians, including Cheyenne and settler women, children, and elders. The tribe began raiding emigrant settlements and military and trading posts on a wide front after the Sand Creek Massacre (1864), in which a peaceful Cheyenne village was destroyed by the U.S. cavalry. In the Treaty of Medicine Lodge (1867), the Southern Cheyenne were assigned a reservation in Oklahoma, but they settled there only after 1875. After George Armstrong Custer's attack on their Washita River village in 1868, the Southern Cheyenne were fairly peaceful until 1874–75,

DULL KNIFE

*(b. c. 1810, Rosebud River, Montana Territory [U.S.]—d. 1883, Tongue
River Indian Reservation, Montana Territory)*

Dull Knife (as he was called by the Sioux) was a chief of the
northern Cheyenne who led his people on a desperate trek from
confinement in Indian Territory (Oklahoma) to their home in
Montana. He was known to his people as Morning Star.

Five months after Lieut. Col. Custer's defeat at the Battle
of the Little Big Horn, the cavalry, on a punitive expedition,
attacked Dull Knife's camp on the Red Fork of Powder River
(Nov. 25–26, 1876). Most of his tribe escaped, but their shelters,
clothing, blankets, and stores of food were destroyed. By the
time that Dull Knife surrendered to the army, many of his people
had succumbed to starvation or exposure. In 1877 the U.S. Army
sent him and his tribe to a reservation of southern Cheyenne
in Indian Territory. The land was unprofitable, there was little
food, and the climate was unhealthy. Within two months of their
arrival in Oklahoma, two-thirds of the tribe were sick and many
died. Dull Knife and other exiled northern Cheyenne leaders
pleaded for a reservation for their people in their former territory, but to no avail.

Fearing that his tribe would die out, Dull Knife, along with
Little Wolf, a war chief of the northern Cheyenne, determined
to go home, despite army opposition. On Sept. 9, 1878, he and
Little Wolf led what was left of their people from the reservation. Their combined band consisted of 89 warriors and 246
women and children. They traveled more than 400 miles (644
km), managing to defeat or elude the various army detach-
ments sent to bring them back (more than 10,000 soldiers were
employed for this task). In October the Cheyenne crossed the
South Platte River of Nebraska, and the followers of Little Wolf
and Dull Knife separated. (Little Wolf's band headed northwest,
surrendered to the army on March 25, 1879, and was allowed to
remain in Montana.) Dull Knife and his people headed for the
Red Cloud Agency, not knowing it had been discontinued. On

Oct. 23, 1878, he and his people surrendered peaceably to the army and were imprisoned in nearby Fort Robinson (Nebraska). When they refused to return to Oklahoma, an attempt was made (from Jan. 5, 1879) to starve them into submission, and the Indians were deprived of heat, food, and water. They broke out of prison on January 9, and, in their dash for freedom, 64 were killed and 78 were eventually recaptured (most of them wounded). Six people, including Dull Knife and surviving members of his family, escaped and made it to the relative safety of the Pine Ridge Reservation in South Dakota. By this time, public opinion was on the side of the Indians, forcing the Bureau of Indian Affairs to abandon its plans to relocate them. A reservation was established for the northern Cheyenne on the Tongue and Rosebud rivers, where Dull Knife and his people (fewer than 80 remaining) were finally allowed to settle, rejoining Little Wolf's band.

when they joined in the general uprisings of the southern Plains tribes. In 1876 the Northern Cheyenne joined the Dakota in the Battle of the Little Bighorn and there defeated Custer.

Early 21st-century population estimates indicated more than 20,000 Cheyenne descendants.

CADDOAN SPEAKERS

Caddoan languages were spoken from South Dakota to northeastern Texas as well as in Arkansas and northwestern Louisiana. Caddo proper is the only language included in the Southern division of of Caddoan languages. The languages of the Northern branch include Kitsai, Arikara, Pawnee, and Wichita. The cultural roots of Caddoan-speaking peoples lay in the prehistoric mound-building societies of the lower Mississippi River valley.

Participants in an Arikara medicine ceremony stand in line, holding rattles and singing. c. *1908.* Buyenlarge/Archive Photos/Getty Images

ARIKARA

The Arikara (also called Sahnish) were culturally related to the Pawnee, from whom they broke away and moved gradually northward, becoming the northernmost Caddoan tribe. Before American colonization of the Plains, the Arikara lived along the Missouri River between the Cannonball and Cheyenne rivers in what are now the U.S. states of North and South Dakota.

Traditionally, the Arikara lived in earth lodges within substantial semipermanent villages. Their economy relied heavily upon raising maize, beans, squash, sunflowers, and tobacco. Arikara households used these products and traded them with other tribes for meat and processed hides. Arikara women were responsible for farming, food preparation and preservation, clothing production, lodge building, and the rituals associated with their work. Arikara men hunted deer, elk, and buffalo, provided defense, and performed rituals related to these practices.

The most important items in Arikara material culture were the sacred bundles. These collections of objects were treated as living connections to the divine, and many village activities were organized around the perceived needs of the bundles and the sacred beings who communicated through them. Each bundle had a bundle-keeper, an office that tended to be the hereditary prerogative of a few leading families. Lower leadership positions were associated with organized military, dancing, and curing societies. The Arikara shared with other Plains tribes the practice of self-sacrifice in the Sun Dance.

The Arikara were seen as an obstacle by white trading parties moving up the Missouri River. In 1823 a battle with traders under the aegis of William H. Ashley's Rocky Mountain Fur Company resulted in the first U.S. Army campaign against a Plains tribe. In response, the Arikara left their villages and adopted a nomadic equestrian lifestyle for a period of years.

Although the Arikara had numbered between 3,000 and 4,000 individuals near the end of the 1700s, wars and epidemics had severely reduced their population by the middle of the 19th century. In the 1860s they joined the Mandan and Hidatsa tribes. Together these tribes formed a unit, becoming known as the Three Affiliated Tribes, and a reservation was created for them at Fort Berthold, N.D. By 1885 the Arikara had taken up farming and livestock production on family farmsteads dispersed along the rich Missouri River bottomlands.

In the 1950s construction of the Garrison Dam flooded the bottomlands, creating Lake Sakakawea. More than a quarter of the Fort Berthold reservation lands were permanently flooded by the rising waters. This and the discovery of oil in the Williston Basin forced another removal, this time to new homes on the arid North Dakota uplands, where farming was difficult. As a result, reservation communities suffered an economic depression. By the end of the 20th century, however, the Three Affiliated Tribes had regained a level of prosperity through buffalo ranching and other tribal businesses.

Early 21st-century population estimates indicated more than 1,000 individuals of Arikara descent.

PAWNEE

The Pawnee lived on the Platte River in what is now Nebraska, U.S., from before the 16th century to the latter part of the 19th century. In the 19th century the Pawnee tribe was composed of relatively independent bands: the Kitkehahki, Chaui, Pitahauerat, and Skidi. Each of these bands occupied several villages, which were the basic social unit of the Pawnee people.

The Pawnee traditionally lived in large, dome-shaped, earth-covered lodges during most of the year, opting for tepees while on bison hunts, as was the case with many other Plains Indians. Pawnee women raised maize, squash, and beans and were practiced in the art of pottery making. Horses were first introduced in the 17th and 18th centuries from Spanish settlements in the Southwest.

Chiefs, priests, and shamans were held in highest esteem among the Pawnee. Each chief of a village or band had in his keeping a sacred bundle. Shamans were believed to possess special powers to treat illness and to ward off enemy raids and food shortages. Priests were trained in the performance of rituals and sacred songs. Along with shamanistic and hunt societies, the Pawnee also had military societies.

The traditional religion of the Pawnee included the belief that some of the stars were gods. The Pawnee performed rituals to entreat the presence of these gods, and they also used astronomy in practical affairs (e.g., to determine when to plant crops). Maize was regarded as a symbolic mother through whom the sun god bestowed his blessing. Other important deities were the morning and evening stars and Tirawa, the supreme power who created all these. For a time Pawnee religion included the sacrifice of a captive adolescent girl to the morning star, but this practice ended in the 19th century.

Relations between the Pawnee and settlers were peaceful, and many Pawnee individuals served as scouts in the U.S. Army of the Frontier. The Pawnee nation ceded most of its land in Nebraska to the U.S. government by treaties in 1833, 1848, and 1857. In 1876 their last Nebraska holdings were given up, and they were moved to Oklahoma, where they remained.

Early 21st-century population estimates indicated some 4,500 individuals of Pawnee descent.

WICHITA

The Wichita originally lived near the Arkansas River in what is now the U.S. state of Kansas. They were encountered by the Spanish in the mid-16th century and became the first group of Plains Indians subject to missionization.

Like most Caddoans, the Wichita traditionally subsisted largely by farming maize, pumpkins, and tobacco. Buffalo hunting was also an important part of their economy. Except during hunting expeditions, they lived in communal lodges resembling haystacks and constructed of poles and thatch. On hunting expeditions they resided in tepees. More given to tattooing than most Plains Indians, they were known by other groups as the "tattooed people." They performed a ceremonial dance resembling the Busk, or Green Corn, festivals of the Southeastern tribes, which celebrated first fruits and new fire at midsummer.

In the late 18th century the Wichita moved south, probably under pressure from tribes to the northeast that were encroaching on Wichita territory. By 1772 they were located near what is now Wichita Falls, Texas. During the American Civil War they returned to Kansas, and in 1867 they were removed to a reservation in Oklahoma. Their estimated population in 1780 was 3,200. Wichita descendants numbered more than 1,900 in the early 21st century.

SPEAKERS OF OTHER LANGUAGES

The remaining languages of the Plains were spoken by isolated speakers of Athabaskan, Kiowa-Tanoan, and Uto-Aztecan. These were joined by Michif, a trade language, and Plains Indian sign language. Most of the speakers of Athabaskan are considered to be a part of the Subarctic culture area, though some can be found in the Northwest Coast area and still others in the Southwest. The small Kiowa-Tanoan family of languages also are spoken in New Mexico. Languages of the large Uto-Aztecan family are widely spoken in Mexico, northern Guatemala, and, by fewer numbers, in California, the Great Basin, Arizona, and Oklahoma.

KIOWA (KIOWA-TANOAN)

The Kiowa are believed to have migrated from what is now southwestern Montana into the southern Great Plains in the 18th century. Numbering some 3,000 at the time, they were accompanied on the migration by Kiowa Apache, a small southern Apache band that became closely associated with the Kiowa. Guided by the Crow, the Kiowa learned the technologies and customs of the Plains Indians and eventually formed a lasting peace with the Comanche, Arapaho, and Southern Cheyenne. The name Kiowa may be a variant of their name for themselves, Kai-i-gwu, meaning "principal people."

Powerful and tenacious warriors, the Kiowa and their allies were among the last of the Plains tribes to yield to the U.S. Cavalry. Since 1868 they have shared a reservation with the Comanche between the Washita and Red rivers, centring on Anadarko, Oklahoma. Before their surrender, Kiowa culture was typical of nomadic Plains Indians. After they acquired horses from the Spanish, their economy focused on equestrian bison hunting. They lived in large tepees and moved camp frequently in pursuit of game. Kiowa warriors attained rank according to their exploits

in war, including killing an enemy or touching his body during combat.

Traditional Kiowa religion included the belief that dreams and visions gave individuals supernatural power in war, hunting, and healing. Ten

Kiowa calendar painting of the years 1833–92 on buffalo hide, photograph by James Mooney, 1895. "Seventeenth Annual Report of the Bureau of American Ethnology to the Smithsonian Institution, 1895-96," by James Mooney.

N. SCOTT MOMADAY

(b. Feb. 27, 1934, Lawton, Okla., U.S.)

The Native American author Navarre Scott Momaday wrote many works centred on his Kiowa heritage. Momaday grew up on an Oklahoma farm and on reservations where his parents were teachers. He attended the University of New Mexico (A.B., 1958) and Stanford University (M.A., 1960; Ph.D., 1963), where he was influenced by the poet and critic Yvor Winters. Momaday's first novel, *House Made of Dawn* (1968), is his best-known work. It narrates, from several different points of view, the dilemma of a young man returning home to his Kiowa village after a stint in the U.S. Army. The book won the 1969 Pulitzer Prize for fiction.

Momaday's limited-edition collection of Kiowa folktales entitled *The Journey of Tai-me* (1967) was enlarged with passages of Kiowa history and his own interpretations of that history as *The Way to Rainy Mountain* (1969), illustrated by his father, Alfred Momaday. Native American traditions and a deep concern over human ability to live in harmony with nature permeate Momaday's poetry, which he collected in *Angle of Geese and Other Poems* (1974) and *The Gourd Dancer* (1976). *The Names: A Memoir* (1976) tells of his early life and of his respect for his Kiowa ancestors. In 1989 he published his second novel, *The Ancient Child*, which weaves traditional tales and history with a modern urban Kiowa artist's search for his roots. Later books include *In the Presence of the Sun: Stories and Poems, 1961–1991* (1992), *Circle of Wonder: A Native American Christmas Story* (1994), *The Man Made of Words: Essays, Stories, Passages* (1997), and *In the Bear's House* (1999), a collection of paintings, poems, and short stories that examines spirituality among modern Kiowa. In 2007 a collection of three plays was published, and another volume of poetry, *Again the Far Morning: New and Selected Poems*, was issued in 2011. He was awarded the National Medal of Arts in 2007. Many of his early works were reissued in the 21st century.

medicine bundles, believed to protect the tribe, became central in the Kiowan Sun Dance. The Kiowa and the Comanche were instrumental in spreading peyotism.

The Kiowa were also notable for their pictographic histories of tribal events, recorded twice each year. Each summer and winter from 1832 to 1939, one or more Kiowa artists created a sketch or drawing that depicted the events of the past six months. In the early years of this practice, the drawings were made on dressed skins, while artists working later in the period drew on ledger paper. The National Anthropological Archives of the Smithsonian Institution contain a number of these extraordinary drawings.

Early 21st-century population estimates indicated more than 12,000 individuals of Kiowa descent.

MÉTIS

The Métis are an indigenous nation of Canada that has combined Native American and European cultural practices since at least the 17th century. Their language, Michif (also called French Cree, or Métis), is a French and Cree trade language. The first Métis were the children of indigenous women and European fur traders in the Red River area of what is now the province of Manitoba. They cultivated a distinctive way of life. Their culture, particularly their clothing, artwork, music, and dance, can be characterized as colourful and unique.

In the 21st century, Michif was spoken by some 800 individuals in the United States (Turtle Mountain Reservation, North Dakota) and Canada (scattered locations). The word *métis*, which means "mixed" in French, can be used of any aboriginal (First Nation) person of mixed descent, but the Métis who are of mixed French

LOUIS RIEL

*(b. Oct. 23, 1844, St. Boniface, Assiniboia [western Canada]—d. Nov.
16, 1885, Regina, District of Assiniboia, Northwest Territories, Can.)*

Louis Riel was the leader of the Métis people of western Canada.

Riel grew up in the Red River Settlement in present-day
Manitoba. He studied for the priesthood in Montreal (though
he was never ordained) and worked at various jobs before returning to Red River in the late 1860s. In 1869 the settlement's
Métis population was alarmed by arrangements to transfer the
territorial rights of their settlement from the Hudson's Bay
Company to the Dominion of Canada. They were especially
worried about the expected influx of English-speaking settlers
that this transfer would bring. Riel became spokesman for the
Métis insurgents, who managed to halt the Canadian survey-
ors and prevent the governor-designate, William McDougall,
from entering Red River. They then seized Fort Garry (now
Winnipeg), the headquarters of the Hudson's Bay Company, and
established a provisional government with Riel as president to
negotiate acceptable terms of union with Canada.

During the insurgency, Riel's government court-martialed
and executed Thomas Scott, an English-speaking Canadian,
because he had been strongly opposed to the insurgency. Scott's
death was used as a symbol to stir up hostility in Ontario toward
the Métis. In 1871 Riel urged his followers to join with other
Canadians in repulsing a threatened attack by American Fenians
(Irish revolutionaries), for which he received public thanks.
In 1873 he was elected a member of the Dominion Parliament
for Provencher (a federal electoral district in Manitoba), but,
though he took the oath in Ottawa, he did not assume his seat.
The following year he was expelled from the House but was
quickly reelected for Provencher. In 1875 Riel reported having
a holy vision that called him to become a prophet for the Métis,
who were identified as a people favoured by God. This claim and
Riel's other behaviour concerned some of his followers, who
committed him to a mental hospital in Quebec in 1876. He was

released the following year. In 1879 he moved to Montana and later married and started a family.

In 1884 a delegation of Métis from the Northwest Territories appealed to Riel to represent their land claims and other grievances to the Canadian government. He returned to Canada, and, though he tried to proceed through legal means, he later established a provisional government (March 1885). A brief armed uprising followed, but this was quickly crushed by the military might of the Canadian government, and Riel surrendered. He was tried in Regina, found guilty of treason, and hanged. His death led to fierce outbreaks of ethnic and religious disagreement in Quebec and Ontario, helping to galvanize French Canadian nationalistic opposition to the federal government.

and Cree descent are the only speakers of Michif. There are several varieties of Michif in Canada.

The Métis resisted the Canadian takeover of the Northwest in 1869. Fearing the oncoming wave of settlers from Ontario, the Métis established a provisional government under the leadership of Louis Riel (1844–85). In 1870 this government negotiated a union with Canada that resulted in the establishment of the province of Manitoba. In 2003 Canada recognized the Métis as an indigenous group with the same broad rights as other First Nations peoples.

In the early 21st century the estimated number of Métis was more than 300,000.

SARCEE

During the 18th and 19th centuries, the Sarcee (Sarsi), whose language is of Athabaskan stock, lived near the upper Saskatchewan and Athabaska rivers in the present provinces of Alberta and Saskatchewan, Can. They

PLAINS INDIAN SIGN LANGUAGE

Plains Indian sign language (PISL) was also called Hand Talk. It was a system of fixed hand and finger positions symbolizing ideas, the meanings of which were known to the majority of the tribes of the area. In addition to aiding communication among the deaf, PISL was used by for a broad range of interactions — for hunting and other activities where silence or secrecy might be desirable and for trade between Native Americans who did not speak mutually intelligible languages as well as between Indians and Euro-Americans. It was used at all levels of society. Its occasional misinterpretation was responsible for some confusing name assignments, as among the Hidatsa and Atsina (both of whom came to be called Gros Ventres). Footage from the National Archives made in 1930 that records several varieties of PISL is available on the Internet.

probably moved southward to this region near the end of the 17th century when they became the northern neighbours of the Blackfoot peoples, from whom they received some protection from enemies.

The Sarcee, who call themselves Tsuu T'ina, adopted several aspects of Blackfoot culture, including military societies and the Sun Dance. As hunting and gathering provided them with sustenance, tobacco was their only crop, and it was planted with much ceremony. The Sarcee suffered from continual attacks by the Cree and other tribes. Their population was reduced further by epidemics of smallpox and scarlet fever in the 19th century. Having drawn together during the hardships of the 19th century, the Sarcee, Blackfoot, and Alberta Assiniboin ceded their hunting grounds to the dominion government of Canada in 1877 and took residence on a reservation in Alberta in 1880.

Early 21st-century population estimates indicated some 1,000 Sarcee descendants.

WIND RIVER SHOSHONE AND COMANCHE

The Wind River Shoshone of western Wyoming and the related Comanche of western Texas are usually treated with the larger groups in the Great Basin culture area, The Comanche are a comparatively recent offshoot of the Wind River group. Both Shoshone and Comanche are members of the Uto-Aztecan family. Shoshone dialects were so similar that speakers from the extreme ends of Shoshone territory were mutually intelligible.

Like the Northern Shoshone, the Wind River Shoshone probably acquired horses as early as 1680, before the Spanish occupied their lands. They formed loosely organized bands of mounted buffalo hunters and warriors and adopted many Plains Indian cultural traits such as the use of tepees and the importance of counting coup as a war honour. Sacagawea, who acted as interpreter and guide for the Lewis and Clark Expedition of 1804–06, may have been a member of the Wind River Shoshone.

CONCLUSION

Most of the Native Americans of the Plateau and Plains had been pushed west or south by white settlement or stronger groups. As a result, their economies changed, sometimes considerably, as when the horse was introduced to the Plains. Ultimately, though, they lost the freedom to roam and were limited to designated lands. In this circumstance, their noted ability to adapt quickly served them well, at least in the natural world. They had not been so fortunate when dealing with superior firepower or with microbes to which they had no immunity.

Once they were no longer able to resist confinement to reservations, new betrayals and indignities arose. Not only was much of their treaty-gained land stolen or taken from them by trickery, but their cultures were denigrated and assaulted, their languages often lost to future generations. Yet, despite the attempts to Christianize and assimilate them into the dominant Euro-American culture, the native peoples of the Plateau and Plains have endured. They have rejected the romantic notion of the Noble Savage, struggling against all odds to carry on and stay true to what remains of their heritage. The descendants of the Plateau and Plains people, like their counterparts in other culture areas, have learned to fight on a different battlefield: the Canadian and U.S. courts of law.

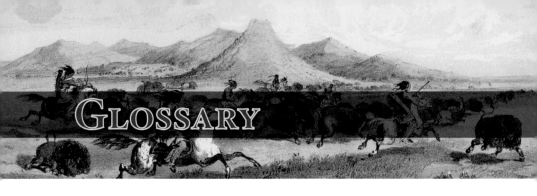

GLOSSARY

abrogate To abolish by authoritative, official, or formal action.

accede Agree; assent.

acumen Keenness of perception, especially in practical matters.

alliteration The use of the same sound, usually a consonant, at the beginning of neighbouring words in a sentence or phrase.

animism A religious belief that everything on Earth is imbued with a powerful spirit, capable of helping or harming human needs.

annuity Derived from the Latin *annuus*, meaning "yearly," an annuity is a sum of money payable yearly (or at other regular intervals).

avatar An incarnation in human form.

Badlands Barren region covering some 2,000 sq miles (5,200 sq km) of southwestern South Dakota.

Chinook North American Indians of the Northwest Coast who spoke Chinookan languages and traditionally lived in what are now Washington and Oregon.

deify To make a god of.

ethnography The study and systematic recording of human cultures.

ethnologist Scientist who deals with the division of human beings into races and their origin, distribution, relations, and characteristics.

ethos The guiding beliefs, standards, or ideals that characterize or pervade a group, a community, a people, or an ideology.

extant Still existing.

habeas corpus A protection against unjust imprisonment that requires a person to be brought before a judge or court for the purpose of being formally charged or released.

hogan Six- or eight-sided home made from wood and covered with earth built by the Navajo.

intermontane Situated between mountains.

longhouse A long, rectangular domicile favoured by indigenous peoples of the American Northeast.

menses Menstrual flow.

millenarian An apocalyptic expectation of a new heaven and earth.

moiety One of two approximately equal portions.

mores The moral attitudes and customs of a given group or society.

Paiute American Indian people originally of Utah, Arizona, Nevada, and California.

palisade A structure erected for defence, consisting of several stakes placed in the ground in a fence-like formation.

phratry A tribal subsection based on the division of clans.

potlatch A ceremony marking a special occasion where the social status of members of Northwest native tribes was established or announced by the giving of gifts.

privation The state of being deprived; especially the lack of what is needed for existence.

pueblo The communal, multistoried dwelling used by native peoples of the American Southwest.

ribald Crude, offensive, or coarse.

shaman A religious figure who uses magic to intercede between the natural and supernatural spheres.

steppe A mid-latitude cold-and-dry region in which there is usually a winter drought. The region covers

the Great Plains, much of the Great Basin, and portions of the Columbia and Snake river plateau.

stigmata Bodily marks or pains resembling the wounds
of the crucified Jesus.

syncretic The fusion of different systems of belief, as in
religion or philosophy.

trade language A restructured language (as a lingua
franca or pidgin) used especially in commercial
communication.

travois A mode of transport consisting of two joined
poles and a platform attached to both and draped
between them that is dragged, most often by a horse
or dog.

watershed A land area in which all precipitation flows
into a single river system.

wickiup A dome-shaped form of lodging favoured by
Northeastern Native American peoples, constructed
by draping bent saplings with rushes or bark; also
called a wigwam.

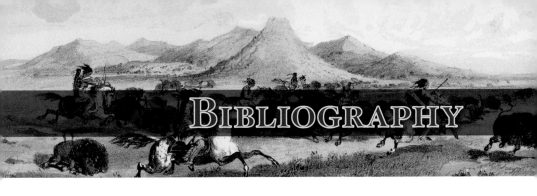

Although there is no broad synthesis of traditional Plateau cultures, essays considering the cultures and history of the region may be found in William C. Sturtevant (ed.), *Handbook of North American Indians*, vol. 12, *Plateau*, ed. by Deward E. Walker, Jr. (1998).

Books on single tribes include James A. Teit, *The Thompson Indians of British Columbia* (1900, reprinted 1975); Herbert Joseph Spinden, *The Nez Percé Indians* (1908, reprinted 1974); and Verne F. Ray, *The Sanpoil and Nespelem: Salishan Peoples of Northeastern Washington* (1933, reprinted 1980).

Historical analyses of Plateau peoples and cultures include Larry Cebula, *Plateau Indians and the Quest for Spiritual Power, 1700–1850* (2003); and Lillian A. Ackerman, *A Necessary Balance: Gender and Power Among Indians of the Columbia Plateau* (2003).

Regional syntheses of the traditional cultures of the Plains include Robert H. Lowie, *Indians of the Plains* (1954, reprinted 1982), a classic work; Peter Iverson (ed.), *The Plains Indians of the Twentieth Century* (1985); William C. Sturtevant (ed.), *Handbook of North American Indians*, vol. 13, *Plains*, ed. by Raymond J. DeMallie, 2 vol. (2001); and Loretta Fowler, *The Columbia Guide to American Indians of the Great Plains* (2003). Patricia Albers and Beatrice Medicine, *The Hidden Half: Studies of Plains Indian Women* (1983), is one of the first scholarly collections written about and by Native American women.

The artistic and material traditions of the Plains are discussed in a number of richly illustrated volumes, such as George C. Frison, *Prehistoric Hunters of the High Plains*, 2nd ed. (1991); Evan M. Maurer, *Visions of the People: A Pictorial History of Plains Indian Life* (1992); Candace S. Greene and Russell Thornton (eds.), *The Year the Stars Fell: Lakota Winter Counts at the Smithsonian* (2007); and Michael Bad Hand Terry, *Daily Life in a Plains Indian Village, 1868* (1999), a volume that includes photos of rare items such as 19th-century sunglasses. Prehistoric and early historic material culture are the focus of Stanley A. Ahler and Marvin Kay (eds.), *Plains Village Archaeology: Bison Hunting Farmers in the Central and Northern Plains* (2007).

Ethnographic and historic analyses of equestrian peoples other than the Sioux nations include John C. Ewers, *The Blackfeet* (1958, reissued 1988); Paul C. Rosier, *Rebirth of the Blackfeet Nation, 1912–1954* (2001); Robert H. Lowie, *The Crow Indians* (1935, reprinted 1983); George Bird Grinnell, *The Cheyenne Indians*, 2 vol. (1923, reprinted 1972); Loretta Fowler, *Arapahoe Politics, 1851–1978* (1982), and *Shared Symbols, Contested Meanings: Gros Ventre Culture and History, 1778–1984* (1987); Ernest Wallace and E. Adamson Hoebel, *The Comanches* (1952, reissued 1988); Morris W. Foster, *Being Comanche: A Social History of an American Indian Community* (1991); Gerald Betty, *Comanche Society: Before the Reservation* (2002); and Jacki Thompson Rand, *Kiowa Humanity and the Invasion of the State* (2008).

The many Sioux groups are considered in Gordon MacGregor, *Warriors Without Weapons* (1946, reprinted 1975), a study of the society and personality of the Teton Dakota under reservation conditions; Richard Erdoes, *Crying for a Dream: The World Through Native American Eyes* (1990), focusing on Sioux religious ceremonies; Paul B. Steinmetz, *Pipe, Bible, and Peyote Among the Oglala Lakota: A Study in Religious Identity* (1980, reissued 1990); Marla N. Powers, *Oglala Women: Myth, Ritual, and Reality* (1986);

Thomas Constantine Maroukis, *Peyote and the Yankton Sioux: The Life and Times of Sam Necklace* (2004); and Jeffrey Ostler, *The Plains Sioux and U.S. Colonialism from Lewis and Clark to Wounded Knee* (2004).

Accounts of village tribes include Alfred W. Bowers, *Mandan Social and Ceremonial Organization* (1950, reprinted 1991), and its companion volume, *Hidatsa Social and Ceremonial Organization* (1965, reissued 1992); Roy W. Meyer, *The Village Indians of the Upper Missouri: The Mandans, Hidatsas, and Arikaras* (1977); Alice C. Fletcher and Francis La Flesche, *The Omaha Tribe*, 2 vol. (1911, reissued 1992); Terry P. Wilson, *The Underground Reservation: Osage Oil* (1985), a detailed tribal history, despite its title; W. David Baird, *The Quapaw Indians: A History of the Downstream People* (1980); and Robin Ridington and Dennis Hastings, *Blessing for a Long Time: The Sacred Pole of the Omaha Tribe* (1997).

INDEX